NEWS
FROM
NEWMARKET

D. Occomore

IAN HENRY PUBLICATIONS

ISBN 0 86025 513 1

Published by
Ian Henry Publications, Ltd.,
20 Park Drive, Romford, Essex RM1 4LH
and printed by
L.P.P.S. Ltd., 128 Northampton Road, Wellingborough NN8 3PJ

Acknowledgements

I would like to thank the staff at the Cambridge Collection for their help with my queries and the access to the newspaper collections. To the staff of the Suffolk Record Office and BT Archive. To Newmarket Local History Society for their invaluable help and access to their local history archive. To the Newmarket Central Library for access to the racing collection. And finally to Mrs Joan Shaw for casting her expert eye over my historical footnotes.

Theatre, Newmarket.

On Saturday, Octr. 31st. 1807. a (*never performed here*,) a Musical Piece, In Three Acts, called The

Three and the Deuce.

Pertinax Single, Mr. FISHER
Peregrine Single, Mr. FISHER
Percival Single, Mr. FISHER
Mr. Milford, Mr. REYMES--Justice Touchit, Mr. PASTON
Humphrey Grizzle, Mr. FISHER Jun.--Frank, Mr. SCRAGGS Jun.
Mac Floggan, Mr. G. FISHER--Renard Mr. C. FISHER
Cramp, Mr. HIGH--Pinch. Mr. J. FISHER--Tippy, Master SCRAGGS.
Miss Milford, Miss NEWMAN--Phebe, Mr. G. FISHER
Taffline, Mrs. SCRAGGS.

To which will be added, the Grand Melo Dramatic, Allegorical Spectacle, of

CINDERELLA;

Or, The Little Glass Slipper.

With New Scenery, Dresses, and Decorations.

Prince, Mr. FISHER Jun.--Cupid, Master W. SCRAGGS-Hymen, Master SCRAGGS
Lords, Messrs REYMES, PASTON, SCRAGGS, &c. Pedro, Mr. J. FISHER.
Venus, Mrs. SCRAGGS--Nymphs, Mrs G. FISHER. &c. &c.
Vixenella, Mrs. FISHER--Spitefulnella, Miss NEWMAN--Cinderella, Miss FISHER.
Genii, Graces, Attendants, Pages, &c. &c.
The following are Sketches [in Part] of the Scenery.
Morning's Dawn discovering the Rosy Retreat of Venus. Cupid arrives sailing on his Quiver, He Grinds his Arrows, Figure of Cinderella on the Sea. Nymphs entangle the Prince in a Silver Net. Cupid wounds Him, He becomes enamoured of the Figure which vanishes from his sight. The Prince disgusted with the Statue of Diana, (to whom he has been a constant Votary till wounded by Cupid,) orders it from his Presence.

Cinderella's Kitchen,

Two Lizards, Four Rats, A Pumpkin and Dresser, are Changed to Footmen, Chariot, &c. in which Cinderella is escorted to the

PRINCE's BALL ROOM.

Cupid indulgent to Cinderella, puts back the Clock. Time indignant puts it forward. A DANCE, by the Prince and Cinderella, her hasty retreat and loss of the Slipper The PROCLAMATION of the Prince, who desires for his Wife her whom the Glass Slipper Fits, The Failure of the Candidates in fitting the Slipper.

Love and Virtue Triumphant.

Venus &c. descend in Clouds to the Nuptials of the Prince and Cinderella.

NB. The above Melo Drame being brought out at a very great expence, nothing less than full PRICE can be admitted. Boxes, 3s Pit 2s Gall. 1s Days of Playing next Week, Tuesday, Thursday, and Saturday. J. Fisher, Printer. *Vivant Rex et Regina.*

INTRODUCTION

While in the process of studying local history, I have spent many hours searching in county record offices and in the county libraries local collections, for information about the lives of our ancestors. Many of the deposited records are official documents or accounts compiled by academic researchers. Although these have been extremely useful resources, I have always been more interested in the records left by the less educated - for want of a better name 'the ordinary man and woman', whose stories never made the official records and in the past have not always been recognised as relevant when recalling and recording our history.

Fortunately we live in more enlightened times and we are now recording written and oral evidence of the ordinary lives of men and women. As historians of the 21st century we are very lucky to be able to access a great deal of day to day information about our ancestors from the late 18th century to the present day, because they have left us a wonderful, and largely untapped, written source of daily life in this country - these are, of course, their daily and weekly newspapers.

The newspaper provides us with a window that we can look through, to view daily events as they happen. We can follow stories as they unfold over months and sometimes years. It is these stories that have affected the lives of those who lived in the locality in the past, and sometimes still influence the way we ourselves live today.

Turning over the pages week by week, year by year, we can begin to appreciate what life was like for our ancestors. Every little detail and every blemish was recorded, in fact our ancestors thirst for accuracy has been the gain of the historian, as in many newspapers of this date inaccuracies were publicly corrected in later editions.

The newspapers that I have used to provide the reports about Newmarket in this book were published in Cambridge from the early 19th century. Most of the reports are from *The Cambridge Independent Press* (1815-1981) with some supplementary accounts from the *Cambridge Chronicle* (1762-1934), marked CC in the text. Both papers contained national and county news, and more interestingly for us items referring to Newmarket. The dates will of course be those of the published weekly edition of the paper. During the early years there were very few local stories as the papers were more concerned with national events and political news, although several column inches were devoted to advertisements for local land and estate sales. As the century progressed more and more material of local events in the towns and villages surrounding Cambridge become available and so some editing has been necessary.

Newmarket is a town with two personalities, on the one hand there is the horse racing and all the supporting industry and services that racing requires, and on the other hand the industry and services that could be found in any small size country market town. Obviously there is some cross over between these two facets but on the whole they lead fairly separate lives. When talking of Newmarket, racing is the most well known aspect to be brought to mind, and many books have been written about this side of its life.

Newmarket was not mentioned in the Domesday book as it did not exist in Norman England, it wasn't until 1227 when King Henry III gave Richard Argentein the right to hold a fair at his manor of New Market that the town stepped on to the stage of history. In the Stuart period James I built a palace here and began to use the surrounding countryside for hunting, but modern Newmarket began with Charles II who rebuilt the Royal Palace and indulged in hunting, cockfighting, and of course, horse racing, in 1664 introducing a race for the Town Plate that is still run today. Newmarket has always been a centre for all forms of gambling, but as this book concentrates on the town I have included some of the more unusual non-racing aspects of this side of Newmarket's life.

The town, on the other hand, has a very varied and interesting history of its own; this has not been written about to any great extent. Newmarket's geographical position standing between the high land of Suffolk and the marsh of the Cambridgeshire Fens, as well as straddling the ancient Icknield Way, made the town an the important gateway to East Anglia. In fact, the main roads from the north and south actually converged west of the town and then diverged again on the eastern side. Conversely, there were all the administrative difficulties of the town being part Suffolk and part Cambridgeshire, the actual boundary running down the High Street; St Mary's, the White Hart and the Crown were in Suffolk, with All Saints, the Rutland Arms and the Jockey Club in Cambridgeshire. Again, the position of Newmarket made it an ideal staging post for the mail coaches from London to Norwich, although Newmarket could never be considered as being on a main railway route, considerable rail traffic was dealt with in conjunction with the racing industry, eventually necessitating three stations.

During the first half of the 19th century, several local utilities came into existence; the gas works in 1839/40, the waterworks in 1844, and the railway in 1848. All these events, in Victorian times, would normally have been marked with the board of directors holding a grand dinner at some local venue, but it seems that even if this was the case in Newmarket, these events were not reported in the local press.

Newmarket as the name suggests had two fairs and a weekly market and all the inherent problems of law and order that such institutions produced. To service the inhabitants of the town there were numerous high street shops, workshops, inns, public houses, and even a brewery. The 19th century also heralded speculative building development of terraced houses, especially round the area of the railway station. There were also many large houses built by the aristocracy and gentry for their own use, or as lodgings for the racing. These were often staffed and serviced by the tradespeople of the town.

The period covered in this book was one of development and expansion, not only in population but also in public amenities and services; in fact, Newmarket was a very thriving place in Victorian times.

Dave Occomore 2003

View of Newmarket in 1801

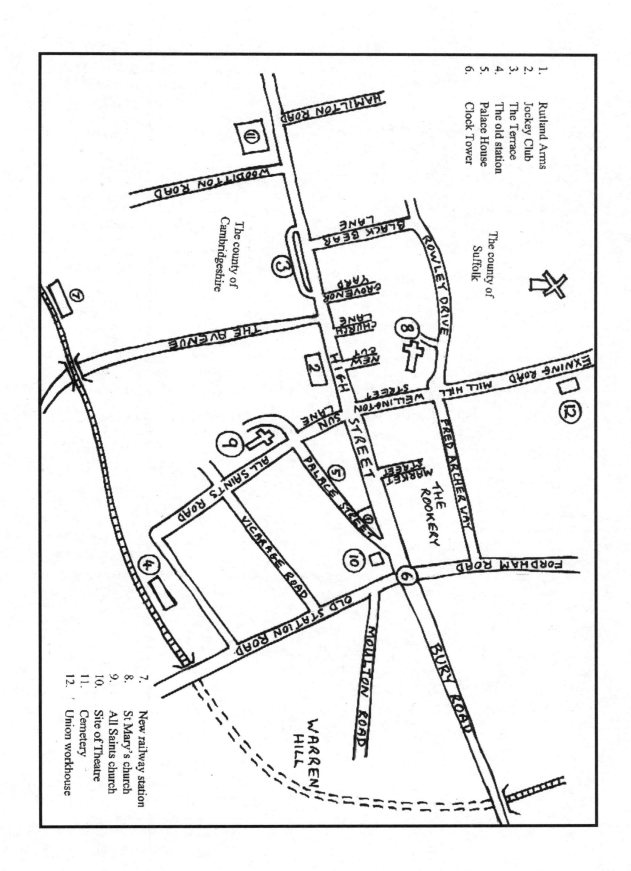

1. Rutland Arms
2. Jockey Club
3. The Terrace
4. The old station
5. Palace House
6. Clock Tower

7. New railway station
8. St Mary's church
9. All Saints church
10. Site of Theatre
11. Cemetery
12. Union workhouse

The county of Cambridgeshire

The county of Suffolk

HAMILTON ROAD

WOODDITTON ROAD

BLACK BEAR LANE

ROWLEY DRIVE

GROVENOR YARD

CHURCH LANE

THE AVENUE

NEW CUT

EXNING ROAD

MILL HILL

WELLINGTON STREET

HIGH STREET

SUN LANE

ALL SAINTS ROAD

VICARAGE ROAD

PALACE STREET

FRED ARCHER WAY

MARKET STREET

THE ROOKERY

FORDHAM ROAD

OLD STATION ROAD

MOULTON ROAD

BURY ROAD

WARREN HILL

3

1800

PLEASANT RESIDENCES and DESIRABLE
FARMS, at or near NEWMARKET,
Late the property of RICHARD VERNON, Esq.;
Deceased
To be SOLD by AUCTION,
By ROBERT ISAACSON,

On TUESDAY, October 28th 1800, between the hours of three and five in the afternoon, at the Ram Inn, Newmarket, Cambridgeshire, in LOTS; All that truly desirable Bricked MANSION HOUSE, with sash front, pleasantly situated on the *Terrace, Newmarket*; comprising 2 parlours, a kitchen, backhouse, pantry, and store room, on the ground floor; 3 good bed chambers, convenient attics, an excellent dry cellar, paved yard, and a pump, well supplied with excellent water; formally in the occupation of Mr John Watson, deceased.

Likewise, a very desirable Bricked and Sash fronted DWELLING HOUSE, adjoining the above; consisting of 2 convenient rooms on the ground floor, 2 good sleeping rooms, and attics over the same.

Immediate possession of both the above premises be had.

Likewise, all that capital MANSION HOUSE, bricked and sash fronted, adjoining the *Coffee-House*, in *Newmarket*; comprising 2 handsome parlours, 2 drawing rooms, kitchens and pantries, etc. 6 excellent sleeping rooms, and a very good cellar; a large yard, with a barn, and stabling for 14 horses; a garden, walled-in and well planted, and a very rich paddock behind the premises. The Mansion House is let to Mrs Bones and Mr Marshall, at £30, per annum; the Paddock to Sir Frank Standish, at £ 15.15s per annum; the Stables, Garden, Barn, and Yards, in hands of the Proprietor... (details of farms in Exning and Moulton)

Printed particulars of the estates, and conditions of sale, may shortly be had at the Rainbow Coffee House, Cornhill, London; Ram, Newmarket; Greyhound, Bury; Rose, Cambridge and Walden; White Hart, Bournbridge; Chesterford Inn; Bear and Crown, Ipswich; White Swan, St Peter's Norwich; Coffee houses, Sudbury; Black Boy, Chelmsford; of Mr John Sawyer, Cheveley, near Newmarket; and of Mr Robert Isaacson, auctioneer and appraiser, Oak Farm, Cowlinge, near Newmarket; where catalogues of the Farming Stock may be had in due time.

The Coffee-House is now the Jockey Club. In 1752 the Jockey Club acquired a fifty-year lease on what was called the Coffee-rooms, before the lease expired Mr 'Jockey' Vernon (members were race horse owners, not riders, and each was known as Mr 'Jockey' followed by the surname) bought the lease. In 1772 an ornamental gateway was built to enclose the betting court, further rebuilding took place in 1832. It may be that the Mr 'Jockey' Vernon was the same person referred to in some of these sale particulars?

Mr Marshall may be Ben Marshall the painter who lived in Newmarket for fifteen years and whose son Lambert Marshall was born in Newmarket in 1810 and followed his father as a painter.

The Ram, Newmarket, stood on the site of the Rutland Arms.

1805

FRANCIS DAWSON, Esq. Deceased. All persons to whom FRANCIS DAWSON, of Newmarket, in the county of Cambridge, Esq., stood indebted at the time of his decease, are requested to send the particulars of their claims to Mr Weatherby, of Newmarket; and all persons who stood to the deceased, are requested to pay the sums due from them respectively, to the said Mr Weatherby, who is authorised by the adminisatrix to receive the same.

Substantial Dwelling-House
To be SOLD by AUCTION,
By ROBERT ISAACSON,

On TUESDAY, May 21, 1805, at the *Five Bells Inn*, NEWMARKET, between the hours of 3 and 5 in the afternoon, subject to such conditions of sale as will be then and there produced, (unless sooner disposed of by private contract);

All that substantial Brick and Tiled DWELLING HOUSE, situate at NEWMARKET, in the county of Suffolk, late in the occupation of Mr Thomas Attfield, veterinary surgeon, deceased; comprising a sitting room and parlour in front, good kitchen, an excellent cellar, three good sleeping-rooms, and commodious ceiled attics, a detached backhouse, paved yard supplied with good water, open stable, four stall stable with granary and hay chamber over, blacksmith's shop and forge, a capacious piece of ground, extending 90 feet in length, and 52 feet in breadth in the narrowest part, viz. From the gable end of the four stall stable to the road.

N.B. This Estate is Freehold, may be entered upon immediately, and is the best situation in Newmarket for the erection of a weighing machine for hay, the getting to and from it being so very convenient.

May be viewed by applying to Mr Josiah Marshall, at the Five Bells, Newmarket, the proprietor, and further particulars had of Mr R Isaacson, Oaks Farm, Cowlinge, near Newmarket.

15th June 1805   CC

By Virtue of an Execution from the High Sheriff,
To be SOLD by AUCTION,
By ROBERT ISAACSON,
On Wednesday June 26 1805, and following days the valuable HOUSEHOLD FURNITURE, China, Glass, Earthenware... and other chattels, of Mr JOHN GRIFFITH, Brazier, Ironmonger, Whitesmith, and Tin-plate worker, at the *Five Bells Inn*, NEWMARKET, Suffolk.

The Furniture comprises good 4 post bedsteads, with handsome chintz, morine, and other furniture; fine bordered geese and other feather beds; blankets, mattresses, quilts, etc., mahogany dining, pillar, card, and pembroke tables; mahogany bureau and chests of drawers; mahogany press bedstead, with glass doors and silk curtains and handsome striped Manchester furniture; handsome 8 day clock in a japanned case; ditto in wainscot ditto; wainscot dining, pillar, and kitchen tables; handsome pier and dressing glasses in guilt and mahogany frames; a handsome set of white and gold breakfast china, china punch bowls, etc.; mahogany night table; easy chair; mahogany chairs, with hair seats; neat-chamber ditto; strong and useful kitchen chairs; and a great variety of other useful and valuable furniture.

The Stock consists of a collection of well chosen tin ware, braziery, and ironmongery goods of every description; likewise several articles in the cutlery line of business, as will appear in catalogues to be had as soon as possible at most of the public houses in the neighbourhood, place of sale, and of Mr R Isaacson, Oaks Farm, Cowlinge, near Newmarket.

Each day's sale to begin at 10 o'clock.

The above is a very desirable situation for any person wishing to engage in the braziery and ironmongery business; and any person of such a situation may be accommodated with the stock by appraisement, on or before *Saturday* the 22nd instant, but not after that time.

A whitesmith was a tradesman who worked in tin and silver.

24th August 1805   CC

ESTATES AT NEWMARKET.
To be SOLD by AUCTION.
By ROBERT ISAACSON,
At the *Five Bells*, in NEWMARKET, on TUESDAY the 10th day of *September*, 1805, precisely at four o'clock in the afternoon, in the following lots;

Lot 1 All that MESSUAGE, TENEMENT, or PUBLIC-HOUSE, situate upon Mill Hill, called the FIVE BELLS, in the occupation of John Griffith; a Messuage or Tenement adjoining, occupied by Wm. Cross; and Two Tenements, in the possession of Mrs Griffith and Mrs Wormell; with the Yards, Gardens, Outhouses, and a Piece of Land adjoining called the Nursery; subject to the Estate for Life of Sarah Griffith, widow, therein.

Lot 2. FOUR TENEMENTS, adjoining lot 1 with the Outhouses and Yard thereto belonging, in the several tenures of ----- Carter, John Mendham, Sarah Lewis, and Wm. Revell.

Lot 3. A Brick and Tiled MESSUAGE, delightfully situated on Mill Hill, with the Garden and Outhouse to the same belonging; in the occupation of Martin Webb.

For further particulars enquire of the Auctioneer, at Oaks Farm Cowlinge, Suffolk; or of Mr COOPER, solicitor, Cambridge.

28th September 1805   CC

Valuable Furniture, Plate, fine Old Port Wine, Brandy, Rum, Etc.
To be SOLD by AUCTION,
By ROBERT ISAACSON.
Upon the premises, on WEDNESDAY, *October* 9 1805 and two following days,

The truly valuable HOUSEHOLD FURNITURE, PLATE, fine old PORT WINE, SPIRITS, and other effects, of the late FRANCIS DAWSON, Esq. of the Terrace, in Newmarket, in the county of Cambridge, comprising excellent sacken bottom lath, post, and test bedsteads, with mahogany and other feet posts, striped fringed, and other furniture, excellent geese feather beds, upwards of 20 mattresses, 50 pair of blankets, quilts, and counterpanes; mahogany dining tables with circular ends and upon claws, mahogany pembroke, card library, writing, and dressing tables; Scotch carpets of very good dimensions; dressing and chimney glasses in guilt and other frames; a very excellent large mahogany wardrobe, with cedar partitions, mahogany bureau's, chest with draws, basin stands, bedside and night tables, mahogany silent waiter and what-not; gentleman's toilet chest; pair of gloves; excellent spring clock, barometer and thermometer; festoon window curtains; several sofas and easy chairs, handsome mahogany vestibule chairs mahogany chairs, with hair seats and brass nails, handsome with-drawing room and chamber ditto; small quantity of plate; upwards of 80 dozen of fine old choice Port Wine and Spirits, likewise a great quantity of kitchen and culinary requisites too numerous to mention; also an excellent mangle, very neat whisky and harness, capital house engine, a most excellent wheat mill and machine for dressing flour, large bathing tub with iron hoops, painted tin warm bath, stone garden roll, several cucumber frames and hand-glasses, sundry other garden utensils, etc. etc. as will appear in catalogues to be had, at 6d, each, of Mr Rogers, bookseller and stationer, Newmarket; Eagle and Child, Cambridge; White Hart, Bournbridge; Bull, Barton Mills; Rose, Walden and Linton; Lamb, Ely; Greyhound, Bury; Chequers, Brandon; Bell, Mildenhall; and of Mr R Isaacson, auctioneer, appraiser and agent to the Royal Exchange Assurance Office, Oaks Farm, Cowlinge, near Newmarket. May be viewed the day preceding the sale from ten until five o'clock.

Each day's sale will begin at ten o'clock, and continue without interruption. N.B. No lots will be delivered on any account during the time of sale.

1807

2ⁿᵈ May 1807   CC

Desirable Situation in the Grocery and Linen-Drapery trade
NEWMARKET, with immediate possession.
To be SOLD by AUCTION
By ROBERT ISAACSON
At the GREYHOUND INN NEWMARKET.

By order of the assignees of James Dove of Newmarket a bankrupt, on Tuesday May 5, 1807 between the hours of 4 and 6 in the afternoon subject to such conditions of sale as will then and there produced unless previously disposed of by private contract of which timely notice will be given.

Lot 1. All that truly desirable brick and sash fronted DWELLING HOUSE, comprising a roomy shop with extensive ware houses, good parlour, kitchen two sleeping rooms, with convenient attics, and small yard behind the dwelling-house, with a good lead pump well supplied with excellent water; late in the occupation of the said James Dove.

The above is copyhold, and has carried on an extensive trade in the aforementioned branches, and may be considerably improved, as the premises adjoin the Corn Market and makes it a very eligible situation for many other trades.

Lot 2 All that desirable Copy hold TENEMENT comprising a kitchen, cellar, most excellent Brake-Office and three sleeping rooms; in the occupation of Eliz Daniels and ~~~ Hart.

There is a good stable adjoining this lot, which is situated opposite lot 1.

The whole may be viewed and particulars had of Mr John Isaacson, on the premises of Mr Marshall, cheesemonger, Cambridge; or Mr Redfern, Dowgate Hill, London; and at the Oaks Farm, Cowlinge near Newmarket.

And on Wednesday May 6 1807 and following days, will be SOLD by AUCTION, upon the premises, the entire STOCK in TRADE, of the said bankrupt.

The Linen and Woollen Drapery consists of a great Variety of woollen cloths, velveteen's, fustians, cords, printed cottons, black cambrics, and calicos, shawls, handkerchiefs, Russia Ducks and linens of every description; large quantity of worsted and cotton hose, gloves, hats of all sizes, camblets, stuffs, flannels, etc. The Grocery consists of upward 450 lbs of prime Congou teas, sugars, spices of all sorts, a quantity of cheese in lots, about 4 bushels of white pease etc. 4 large beams, 3 pair of copper scales and weights, quantity of tea canisters and fixtures in the shop, likewise a great variety of haberdashery. The house hold furniture comprises, an excellent sacken bottom bedstead with mahogany feet posts and fine corded, dainty furniture, post, tent, and bureau bedsteads with Manchester and cotton hangings, very capital borders, geese feather beds, bolsters, and pillows, wool and straw mattresses; about 12 pair of blankets most of them new, counterpanes, sheets and quilts; mahogany dining, pillar, and dressing tables, mahogany chairs with hair seats and brass nails, kitchen and chamber ditto, capital eight day clock in a neat wainscot case, pier and dressing glasses framed and glazed, bureaus, chests of draws, beaufet and cupboards; variety of culinary requisites, china, glass earthenware, etc. kitchen range with wind-up cheeks, bath stoves, washing copper, mash and wort tubs roasting jack; also cart and harness, etc. which will appear in catalogues to be had upon the premises; at the inns in the neighbourhood; of Mr Marshall cheesemonger, Cambridge; and at the Oaks Farm, Cowlinge Newmarket.

Tea and grocery to be sold on the 1st and 2nd days; the 3rd and 4th days haberdashery and hosiery the 5th day, hats, slops, cloths, hosiery, shop fittings, 6th day, woollens, drapery, and mercery and the last day, household furniture. May be viewed three days previous to the sale. On account of the great number of lots, each sale will positively begin at ten o'clock.

16th May 1807   CC

TERRACE NEWMARKET
Valuable Household Furniture, Brussels and other Carpets, rare old and modern French and Indian China, exquisitely fine Bed and Table Linen, Plate, Books etc.
To Be SOLD by AUCTION
By ROBERT ISAACSON,

On Wednesday May 27 1807, and following days (Sunday excepted) upon the premises formerly the residence of the late Richard Vernon, Esq.

All the valuable HOUSEHOLD FURNITURE, Linen, Plate, Books, China, Glass, Earthenware, etc., etc., of Mrs BINFIELD, late of Newmarket, deceased. The Furniture comprises several excellent large bedsteads, with mahogany posts, lath bottoms, and handsome dimity, chintz, and other furniture; fine bordered geese feather beds, superfine Witney and cotton blankets, quilts and counterpanes, large hair and wool mattresses; capital large pier and dressing glasses mahogany chests of drawers, wardrobes, secretaries; cabinet, dining, card, dressing, Pembroke, pillar, and writing tables, bason stands, night tables, etc., chairs with hair seats, japanned chamber chairs;

fine-toned piano-fortes, harpsichord, barrel and wind organ, double-barrelled gun, gentlemen's medicine chest, complete Merlin's weighing machine; a beautiful and most valuable collection of breakfast, table, dresser and ornamental French and India china; about 150 lots of exquisite fine damask and diaper breakfast and table linen, fine Russia and Holland sheets, some of which are four yards long and three wide, wove whole; so large a quantity of real fine linen, the greater part of it never, and the rest little worn, is seldom to be met with. A quantity of new chintz and other best furniture. The plate consists of table, tea, and desert spoons, ladles, knives, forks, candlesticks, etc. The culinary articles are a large quantity of boilers, saucepans, stewpans, etc., etc., a great profusion of glass and earthenware; a copper still with every apparatus. In the coach-house and garden are a neat post-chariot, a quantity of green-house plants, cucumber frames and lights, hand-glasses, lead cisterns, fruit nets, mangle, etc., etc. The whole may be viewed 2 days previous to the sale, between the hours of 11 and 3, with tickets, to be had at the Bank, Newmarket; and catalogues in due time at the Greyhound, Bury; Rose, Cambridge and Walden; Lamb, Ely; Bull, Barton Mills; the Dukes Head, Lynn; Crown, Swaffham; Chequers, Brandon; Bell, Thetford; Coffee House, Sudbury; Peele Coffee House, Fleet street, London; place of sale and of Mr Isaacson, auctioneer and appraiser, Oak Farm, Cowlinge, near Newmarket.

Each day's sale, on account of the great number of lots, to begin at ten o'clock.

On the first day will be sold china, glass, earthenware, and books; second day, linen, plate, and part of the household furniture; third day, music, carriage, green-house plants, and part of the furniture remainder of furniture the following days.

17th October 1807   CC

The long talked of foot race match between Abraham Wood, the celebrated Lancashire pedestrian, and Capt. Barclay, (wherein the former undertook to give the latter 20 miles in a race of 24 hours expected continuance) attracted together the greatest concourse of persons ever seen at Newmarket in the memory of the oldest inhabitant:- The carriages of every description were innumerable, from the batouche and four to a dicky cart, and the horse men and pedestrians all exceeded all accurate estimations of numbers. - The place chosen for the performance of this extraordinary exertion was a single measured mile on the left hand side of the first mile of turnpike road leading from Newmarket to London, towards the Ditch, which mile was roped in, and the competitors both ran on the same ground. ~ They started precisely at eight o'clock on Monday morning. ~ On the previous evening the bets were two to one in favour of the Captain, but within two hours after starting they rather varied in favour of Wood, who, at about twelve o'clock had gone six more miles than his opponent; the exertion of which seemed from that time to have somewhat exhausted his strength, for Capt. Barclay kept gaining upon him, and by two o'clock had redeemed three miles out of the six, which induced Wood to decline all further contest, (some say from indisposition, other think differently.) ~ Wood had run forty miles in six hours, when he gave in, and the Captain having ran three miles and twenty yards after Wood had declined, was declared the victor. ~ From noon time the bets were three to one on the winner. ~ They both ran in flannel jackets and trousers ~ Wood with a yellow silk handkerchief round his head, and Barclay with a flannel cap, exhibiting no very pleasing appearance to the spectators.

Another account says, "Capt. B and Wood started at the appointed time, and both appeared to be in high health and spirits. Wood set off with considerable velocity, which he kept up the whole of the first hour, during which time he went exactly eight miles, in two succeeding hours he slackened his pace a little, going only at the rate of seven miles an hour, consequently at the end of three hours had gone 22 miles. Capt. Barclay set off at a much slower pace than Wood, but he kept it with the greatest exactness, he went almost to a minute six miles an hour. At the end of the first three hours therefore he had gone eighteen miles and Wood had gained four miles. About this time the bets began to turn in favour of Wood. At starting they were three to one in favour of the Captain and there was a kind of general whisper that he was to win: very few people would even take the odds. But when Wood had gained four miles upon his adversary in three hours, the odds against him fell from 3 to 1, to 7 to 4. But during the remainder of the race, Wood's speed and bottom seemed to completely fail him. It was necessary, in order to bring up the 20 miles which he had given Capt. Barclay, that he should gain sixteen miles upon him in the remaining twenty hours: but instead of gaining upon the Captain during the second three hours

he did not even keep pace with him. He stopped twice to rest, and appeared considerably distressed: the second time he stopped he pulled off his shoes and ran without by which means he cut his feet. At length having gone forty miles in six hours and twenty minutes, he declined the contest, and appeared so weak that there was no probability of his gaining it, if he had continued it.

When Wood gave in Capt. Barclay had reduced the four-mile advantage, which Wood gained upon him in the first three hours, to about three miles, and he continued running until he had brought up that distance. Capt. B went during the whole time exactly six miles an hour, and at the conclusion appeared fresh and strong. After he had gone thirty-six miles he stopped and ate heartily. This very unexpected termination of the match has created much dissatisfaction, at least among the losers, and some of them refused to pay the bets. But the general opinion seemed to be that the match was perfectly fair, and that Wood gave up from real fatigue, though upon a former occasion he had gone forty miles, in much less time.

At the close of the race Wood was put to bed in a tent on the ground, from whence he was afterwards removed to the town, and attended by three medical gentlemen. ~ He complained of being seized with pain of his side.
The two Belchers, Ward, Gully, Crib, Gregson, Mendosa: and all the noted prize fighters were on the ground together with such a collection of black-legs as the turf never before witnessed.
It appears that Captain Barclay went on to an even greater achievement two years later, as the prize fighters present Gully and Gregson had connections with Newmarket, Mendoza's forename was Dan, and Jem Belcher kept the Jolly Brewer in Wardour Street, London.
Captain Robert Barclay, who is reputed to have walked 'one thousand miles in one thousand successive hours, at the rate of one mile in each hour'. This extraordinary performance began on Wednesday, 31st May, 1809, at night, when Captain Barclay started his walk half a mile out from the Horse and Jockey, across the Norwich Road over the Heath, and returned. He completed the distance on Wednesday, 12th July at 3-37 pm in the presence of ten thousand spectators. The bet was for a 1,000 guineas a side, and it is supposed that there was no less than 100,000 guineas depending on the event.
John Gully was the son of an innkeeper near Bristol, who later on became a butcher. The business did not prosper, and in 1805 he found himself an inmate of the Fleet Prison for debt. William Pierce, the 'game chicken', came one

day to pay Gully a visit, and there being some boxing-gloves in the room, they whiled away time in a sparring-match in which Gully, who knew something about boxing, showed great proficiency. It occurred to Pierce, then the champion of England, that a means for extricating his pal from debt and prison might be found by arranging a fight; a patron was induced to put up six hundred guineas on behalf of Pierce, while Colonel Mellish, ever ready for sport, backed Gully for four hundred. The creditors were now appeased, and Gully was put into training at Virginia Water. The fight took place at Hailsham, on the Brighton - Lewes road, in the presence of a great assembly, which included the Duke of Clarence, afterwards William IV. The encounter was a desperate one, and at one moment the odds were in favour of Gully, who had a slight advantage in height and reach. Finally, after 64 rounds, lasting an hour and seventeen minutes, had been fought, the experience of the champion began to tell, and Gully, though still game, being reduced to a terrible state, Colonel Mellish withdrew his man, and Pierce retained the championship. In his much shaken condition he grasped Gully's hand, and just found strength enough to articulate before the whole company that he had never fought a better man. After this performance Gully became a great favourite, and later on when Pierce resigned the championship Gully accepted it. For two years no one appeared anxious to meet him; then there came a champion from the north, one Gregson by name; with the result that the great Newmarket fight took place at Six-Mile Bottom, on 14th October, 1807. An encounter of 36 rounds ensued, and in the 24th round the betting was in favour of Gregson, while Gully's chances of winning appeared remote; but both men were so beat that they could hardly stand, and Gully, making a supreme effort, gave Gregson the knock-out. The backers of the defeated man, however, were not satisfied with this result, and a second fight was arranged and took place on 12th May, 1808, at Beechwood, Hertfordshire. It rained in torrents, but this was no damper to the many hundreds who flocked to see the fight. Gregson gave a poor show on this occasion, and Gully asserted his superiority throughout the whole 18 rounds. At the end of the contest Gully told the crowd he would never fight again and became what we now term a Bookmaker. Siltzer.

John Gully, Hare Park. Pigot 1830.

17th October 1807   CC

A gentleman had his pocket picked in the town of Newmarket, on Tuesday, of his pocket book, containing Bank notes, etc amounting to £3500.

The book, with banker's checks to the amount of £1100, has been recovered being thrown in at the window of the post office in Newmarket.

5th April 1809   Bury and Norwich Post

NEWMARKET
FREEHOLD MANSION AND ESTATE
To be SOLD by AUCTION
By Mr Christie
At his Great Room in Pall Mall London, on
Thursday April 27, at 1 o'clock

The very substantial, spacious, and singularly elegant FREEHOLD MANSION, with extensive offices walled gardens with capital hot-houses, pleasure-ground and paddocks, of the late THOMAS PANTON, Esq. well known as an Amateur and Patron of the Turf, deceased situated in and contiguous to the town of Newmarket. This capital residence, for many years the brilliant resort of rank, fashion and elegance, and the marked abode of hospitality and eminent private worth, is every way suited for the resident accommodation of an extensive and splendid establishment. It comprises on the ground floor, in a well-connected range, hall, morning parlour or musick room, boudoir, and bath, dining and drawing rooms, each 36 by 20 feet; library or ball-room, conservatory and saloon, supported by groups of columns; the chief of these apartments open to pleasure grounds of 30 acres, moulded by the hand of nature into beautiful swelling lawns, which command a part of the town of Newmarket and the distant Downs and a rich garden landscape, interspersed with temples, and beset with timber forest trees and thick plantations. Besides the Freehold Land, which compasses a great part of this delightful elysium, are other parcels held for terms, including several inclosures of profitable meadow. The estate is capable of division, but will be offered in one lot, that the Public may not be precluded the opportunity of preserving entire so very desirable a property. May be viewed on Tuesday, April 18, Thursday 20, and Saturday 22, with tickets only, which, with printed particulars, may be had of Edward Weatherby, Esq., Newmarket; and of Mr Christie, Pall-mall.

Thomas Panton was born 1722, in 1766 he was appointed Master of the Game at Newmarket which was an honorary office, but carried with it the Post of Groom of the Removing Wardrobe. He became a member of the Jockey Club in 1753, and won the Derby in 1786 with a horse called 'Noble'. He died in 1809 at the age of 87. In 1809 William Crockford purchased Panton House together with considerable property of at least 50 acres in its rear. Crockford also owned a gambling house on the opposite side of the High Street called, Rothsay House. See Times 20th March & 1st April 1809.

1815

8th September 1815   CC

Newmarket Canal ~ Notice is hereby given, that application is intended to be made in the ensuing session, for leave to bring in a Bill for the purpose of obtaining an Act for making and maintaining a Navigable Cut or Canal, with proper aqueducts, tunnels, feeders, reservoirs, basins, quays, wharfs, warehouses, and other works, from & out of the River Cam, at or near to the end of Burwell Lode, in the parish of Wicken, in the County of Cambridge, to and into the Parish of Newmarket Saint Mary, in the County of Suffolk; which Cut or Canal, and other works, are intended to be made & carried into or through the several parishes, townships, hamlets, or places, of Wicken, Swaffham Prior, Burwell, and Landwade, in the County of Cambridge, and of Exning, and Newmarket Saint Mary, in the County of Suffolk.

Dated this 30th day of August, 1815
PEMBERTON and FISKE. Solicitors

1817

25th April 1817   CC

BUILDING MATERIALS
In the HIGH STREET NEWMARKET,
Being part of the OLD PALACE

To be SOLD by AUCTION, (by the Order of the Lords Commissioners of his Majesty Treasury, and under the direction of the of the Commissioners of his Majesty's Woods, Forests and Land Revenues,)
By Messrs. CREATON & SON
Upon the premises, on TUESDAY the 13th and WEDNESDAY the 14th of May next, at eleven o'clock in the forenoon.
The MATERIALS contained in a considerable extent of BUILDING, part of the said OLD PALACE, to be immediately taken down and cleared away by the purchaser, preparatory to other allotments by Public Sale of the remaining Buildings, and of all the ground; of which

subsequent sale due notice will be given by further advertisement.
The Materials consist of sound brickwork and Plain tilings, Oak and Fir Timber in Roofs, Floors, Shutters, and Doors with Dressings, Wainscoting Staircases, handsome Marble and other Chimney Pieces, Stone Coping, Window Sills. etc.
N.B.~ *The building being the property of the Crown, the purchasers at this sale will not be liable to pay any Auction Duty.*
The premises may be viewed until the days of the sale between the hours of eleven and three (Sundays excepted), by application to Mr W A Arnold, Clerk of the Works, Newmarket, of whom Catalogues may be had at 6d each also at the Office of Woods, etc., Whitehall Place; and at Messrs Creaton and Son's, Great Tower Street.

1819

5th March 1819   CC

From a Correspondent. The old Palace buildings, and other premises, belonging to the Crown, at Newmarket, reported having been sold by private contract, we wish to correct a miss-statement. That the beautiful Residence called the Nunnery is at present not disposed of; altho' it has often been reported in the town (Newmarket) that a gentleman had purchased the same for three hundred pounds ~ a sum too insignificant to mention, and since which the sum of eight hundred pounds has been offered for the same premises. ~ We therefore conclude the estate agents or others belonging to the Revenue department are fully acquainted with the real value of the before mentioned premises, and that both statement may not agree with their estimation, being fully convinced that the department for the disposal of the Crown estates will at these times make the most of Crown property under their control. We therefore hope and trust in times like the present, that not a vestige of property before alluded to may be permitted to escape its utmost value, either to Court parties or others.
The Nunnery, Mr Smallman Francis, gent. 1844 Newmarket Directory: the Nunnery stood near All Saints Church

16th April 1819   CC
NEWMARKET PALACE.
AND THE
ICE-WELL and the Ground thereto adjoining.

To be SOLD by AUCTION.

By Messrs DRIVER.

At the Auction Mart, London, on Tuesday the 20th day of April 1819, at 12 o'clock, in two lots by order of the Commissioners of his Majesty's Woods, Forests and Land Revenues.

A Very IMPROVEABLE FREEHOLD ESTATE, comprising a valuable and extensive Plot of Ground, in the High Street, Newmarket with a portion of the PALACE standing thereon, being a very substantial Building, principally fitted with wainscot and oak, and now completely detached and well inclosed, and comprising a suite of lofty and well-proportioned apartments, with offices on the basement story, and might be most readily converted into excellent Residence for any family of distinction. Also the ICE-WELL and Ground thereto belonging, situate upon Mount Pleasant, in Newmarket. Early possession may be had of the whole.

To be viewed by application upon the premises where printed specifications may be had, also at the Greyhound Inn, and Rutland Arms, Newmarket; at the Castle, Norwich; Angle Bury; Sun, Cambridge; Crown, Hockerill; of James Pillar Esq. Secretary in the Department of Land Revenues, at the office of Woods, Forests, and Land Revenues Whitehall place; of Messrs. Jones and Green, solicitors, Salisbury Square, Fleet Street; at the Auction Mart and Messrs. Driver, surveyors and land agents at their office, No 13, New Bridge Street Blackfriars, London, where a plan of the premises may be seen.

When the building was sold in 1819 most of the palace was pulled down leaving the south-western part of Charles II's building. The two lower floors and the vaulted cellars formed the 19th C house called Palace House Mansion. This advert appears to be the sale of what we now call Palace House and part of the site of the palace that still fronted the High Street where the Congregational Church (now demolished) once stood. Mount Pleasant is now known as Icewell Hill.

23rd April 1819   CC

The Prince Regent has purchased the Palace at Newmarket, which is to undergo a complete renovation under the direction of Mr Nash.

The Prince of Wales inhabited the Palace at various intervals prior to 1791, when he left Newmarket in anger, after that fatal affair with the Jockey Club over the running of one of his horses. His Equerry, Colonel Leigh, continued to live there for some time, and in 1819 the Prince Regent, as he then was, gave orders for the Palace to be thoroughly renovated. When he succeeded to the throne as George IV, he commanded further alterations, which are described in the Sporting Magazine *of 1825:-*

The poor old mutilated palace is also undergoing either repair or improvements, which speaks well for the revival of the Turf. A wall in the front, partly built by King Charles, of brick, and another part by Queen Anne, of brick and stones, is just finished by George IV (or some one else) with flints. There seems a great want of harmony in this... I mean in appearance only... which might have been prevented by re-building the whole. It would not have cost above £13, even if Mr. Hume had lost his seat in Parliament. A screen formed of hurdles stuffed with straw, and secured with hay-bands, has been removed from the front court. This convenient and original thought was intended to separate the Peeresses from the placemen's wives and the publicans' daughters, there being but one entrance. An alteration is about to take place in the grand front of the Palace itself; and the three water-closets recently erected about half-way up, like three cages hung upon a wall, with the conveniences of cisterns, pipes, etc.; very conspicuously placed, are about to be removed; and although one of them is dedicated to the Grand Duke Michael, it will not be spared. According to the plan handed about, if fully acted up to, this Royal Residence will very much resemble a lunatic asylum at Hoxton, but on a much smaller scale; neither are the accommodations for its inmates and attendants equal to those at Hoxton, if we except two or three rooms they have not attempted to improve.

Thus the critics of all times have busied themselves with the poor old Palace! Its final racing occupant was apparently the Duke of Rutland, and in the 1850s it was put up for auction by order of Queen Victoria and the Prince Consort, who are supposed to have dreaded the return of the days of the Royal Turfites. Things were not humming in Newmarket at this time, and it was with great difficulty that the auctioneer obtained a bid from a speculative buyer. The Palace was pulled down shortly afterwards, and on the centre of this property was built a Congregational Church. Siltzer

Palace House

1820

7th April 1820   CC

Fire at Newmarket – On Friday last, during divine service, an alarming fire burst from the premises of Mr Bridgeman, Mill Hill, Newmarket which raged with such violence as to destroy 2 barns, an outbuilding, and 3 cottages, almost instantaneously. By the active exertions of the inhabitants and the Phoenix engine it was prevented spreading farther. It is painful to us to state that the property of the cottagers was for the most part uninsured, and furniture, etc, to a considerable amount were swallowed up in the flames. In this distressing accident we cannot omit noticing the conduct of many ladies, (whose humanity did honour to their hearts,) in spirited exerting themselves and stimulating others in the praise worthy attempts to subdue the devouring element. We understand that a subscription is on foot to relieve the uninsured; on such an occasion, as well as on all others where an appeal is made to benevolence, we are well assured that it will not in vain be made to the generous and humane disposition of the more wealthy inhabitants of Newmarket. This calamity was supposed to be occasioned by a spark from a wheelwright's shop. Such of the property as was insured was mostly in that highly respectable office the Phoenix.
The Phoenix fire office agent was Albertus Pars, who also kept a boarding school for gents. This school was in a house opposite the Terrace in Newmarket High Street, next to The Black Bear.

25th August 1820   CC

This day (Friday) a cricket match will be played at Walden, between eleven gentlemen of that place, and eleven of the Newmarket Club. Stumps to be fixed at 9 o'clock. The match between Bury and Newmarket in the last innings was played with ten men on the part of Newmarket.
Walden refers to Saffron Walden. Another cricket match was recorded as 'a game of cricket was played on the Round Course opposite the grandstand on 17th August 1844' also see February 1851.

1st September 1820   CC

On Friday last a match at cricket was played on Walden Common, between eleven of the Newmarket club, and eleven of Walden, which, contrary to expectations of all parties, terminated in favour of the latter. Betting at the commencement of the match was five to one on the Newmarket gentlemen. State of the game. First Innings Walden 69, Newmarket 54,, second innings Walden 69, Newmarket 24.

1821

14th December 1821   CC

NEWMARKET HEATH TURNPIKE.
Notice is hereby given, that a MEETING of the Trustees of this Turnpike Road will be held at the *Rutland Arms Inn*, Newmarket, on Tuesday the 1st day of January next, at 2 o'clock in the afternoon, to take into consideration the propriety of Erecting a Side-Gate across the Road leading to Dullingham, where it branches from the said Turnpike Road nearly opposite a public house called the White Lion, at the south-west end of the town of Newmarket.
EDWARD WEATHERBY, Clerk to the Trustees.

1824

15th May 1824

On Thursday evening the 6th inst., the neighbourhood of Newmarket was visited with a tremendous storm of thunder, lightning, and rain. The lighting was extremely vivid and forked, and the thunder truly terrific. The company had left the heath about half an hour before it begun, but the fineness of the weather at that time, a numerous party had proceeded to witness the horses' exercise. A torrent of rain unexpectedly burst over their heads, and in the short space of five minutes it had penetrated every garment. Soon after five o'clock, the lightening struck a malt house, the property of Rd Eaton, Esq. at Stetchworth, and in a short time it was enveloped in flames, which extended to a barn, stable, cow-house, and another building. All these were destroyed, and another malting was considerably injured.
Richard Eaton Esq., Stetchworth House. Pigot 1830

1825

15th January 1825

On Saturday last an inquest was taken at Newmarket, before W P Isaacson, gent. coroner,

on view of the body of a young woman, servant to Mr Kendall, surgeon, of that place, whose death was occasioned by a quantity of arsenic which she had purchased at a shop in the town, under pretence of destroying rats, and had taken the previous night. Jealousy of a rival in a love affair is assigned as the cause of this rash act. Verdict, *temporary insanity.*
Norton, Taylor & Kendall, Newmarket Surgeons & Apothecaries. Pigot 1830

1826

11th November 1826

On Saturday last the Norfolk and Suffolk Company opened a splendid New Theatre at Newmarket, with the *Merchant of Venice* and *My Uncle Gabriel.* The house, which is erected on the site of the old building, is replete with every connivance; the internal decoration (by Mr David Fisher) displays the great ingenuity of his pencil; we may without fear of contradiction, say that the brilliancy and beauty of its *tout ensemble* is not surpassed by any provincial theatre in the kingdom. Preceding the Play, an Address, written expressly for the occasion by a gentleman of highly literary and poetic talent in Newmarket, was recited by Mr Fisher. Mr David Fisher played *Shylock* in a manner which might have satisfied the keenest appetite and Mr Charles Fisher fully maintained his reputation as a chaste and refined singer.
David Fisher was born in 1760; after acting at Norwich Theatre Royal, he went into management in April 1792, in partnership with William Scraggs, forming the Norfolk and Suffolk Company of Comedians (only those on stage in London were allowed to be called actors). Their troupe played most of the circuit towns of East Anglia. When Scraggs died in 1808, Fisher accompanied by his whole family and his two brothers' families continued as a company. They made all the scenery and costumes, printed the playbills, and even built theatres. David Fisher died in 1832, though his son Charles (the singer referred to in the report above) continued until a countrywide recession in the theatre led to the closing of the Fisher circuit in 1844. See July 1845 and Dec 1848. This building is in the High Street on Rutland Hill, directly opposite the Waggon and Horses. It has a distinctly angled façade of stucco, with three semi-circular top first floor windows and stands above the old Stuart cockpit.

1831

30th July 1831

Sporting Performance Extraordinary - The wager of 1000 guineas, between Colonel C and Mr Osbaldeston, to ride two hundred miles in ten hours, will come off in October, in the Houghton Meeting at Newmarket. Mr O. will employ about twenty race-horses in the performance, and Newmarket heath will be the ground on which it will be attempted. This we believe is quite a new thing, no such distance having been performed in the same time.

On Saturday of the Houghton Meeting of 1831, excitement again rose to fever pitch over George Osbaldeston's undertaking to ride 200 miles in ten hours on the Heath, for a wager of 1000 guineas a side with Mr Charite. In addition to this, on the Friday night George Osbaldeston [1787-1866] took a bet that he would accomplish this feat in nine hours. He was, on the whole a favourite, though backers of 'Time' were by no means wanting. The morning broke raw and wet, and 'Time' then became a rising favourite. Seven o'clock saw Mr Osbaldeston, Mr Charite, and their two umpires at the Ditch Stand, where only a few spectators had yet gathered together, the watches of the umpires were set and locked up, and at thirteen minutes past seven 'the squire' started on his journey. The course was 4 miles mostly over the Round Course, changing horses on completing each circuit, taking no refreshment till after the 14th round, and then only a mouthful of bread and a little brandy and water. After the 25th round he again had a snack and the 26th round was his fastest, covering 4 miles in 8 minutes, which is remarkable galloping, carrying 11 st. 2 lb. After 120 miles in five hours, eight minutes, and wet to the skin, he dismounted for 6 minutes during which he partook of cold partridge and weak brandy and water. In spite of driving wind and rain, at nine minutes to four, he had won his bets having ridden the 200 miles in eight hours, thirty-nine minutes, including stoppages. Siltzer

30th July 1831

Married - On Thursday last, Mr Thomas Moody jun. hair-dresser, to Miss Last, stay maker, both of Newmarket.
Thomas Moody had his shop in the Market Place. Pigot 1839

1832

28th January 1832

An extraordinary accident happened to the coachman of the Newmarket mail about a fortnight ago, as he was driving through Epping from London towards Norwich, a waggon laden with straw, and having a ladder chained across behind it which protruded some way beyond the side of the wagon, met the coach, but in consequence of the fog and the steam from the horses the coachman could not see it coming; the protruding part of the ladder caught the iron that supports the coach box and cut it through in an instant; the coachman and a gentleman with him on the box were precipitated to the ground and were trodden on by the wheelers, but luckily the horses stopped instantly, and they escaped with a few bruises only.

The usual route of the London to Newmarket coach road was by Epping, Bishop's Stortford and Chesterford, and the coaches generally changed horses at these stages; but occasionally they dropped the Bishop's Stortford passengers at Hockerill. Siltzer.

Although the mail coaches were very regular even having the tollgates opened for them so they did not have to stop, they could also succumb to the weather. On 11th February 1808 when a heavy snow storm, by which the roads were for a time made impassable, the Newmarket mail coach did not get through in five days (The Norfolk and Norwich Remembrancer 1822).

In 1814 the London to Norwich Via Newmarket was described as a 1st Class coach, these are regular patent mails carrying 4 inside and 2 outside passengers.

Pigot's Directory of 1839 lists the coaches to Norwich and Bury St Edmunds as 'Royal Mail' from London calls at the Half Moon, Newmarket every morning at three; goes through Bury, Thetford and Attlebrough. The 'Telegraph' calls at the White Hart Inn, every afternoon at two and the 'Magnet' at a quarter past two; both go through Bury, Thetford, Attlebrough, and Wymondham. All these coaches went to London. Looking back to Pigot's directory of 1830, the 'Magnet' and 'Telegraph', that both left the Swan and Rampant Horse in Norwich, missed the stop at Bury, thus reducing the journey by 8 miles.

1834

1st February 1834

Mr Nunn gave a concert at the theatre at Newmarket, on the evening of yesterday, se'night, which was very genteelly attended.

8th February 1834

Female Sheep Stealers. – Two women have been apprehended for this crime in the neighbourhood of Newmarket. After possessing themselves of the sheep, they employed a butcher to kill and dress it. They burnt the skin, and put the meat into pickle; nevertheless the constable hit upon a clue and they were apprehended, and have been committed for trial. The owner of the lost sheep caused the meat to be distributed amongst the poor.

Sheep stealing at this time seemed to be prevalent in the Eastern Counties. In May 1834 the Cambridge Chronicle *reported that despite offering rewards, the crime was increasing both in extant and audacity. This may have been due in part to the introduction of the New Poor Law of 1834 that proposed out door relief be abolished and all relief given in the new Union Workhouses.*

1836

30th April 1836

Newmarket Palace – There are many curious historical documents connected with the town of Newmarket, which notwithstanding its name, show it to be a place of great antiquity. It is first mentioned in 1227 (12 Henry III), and probably took its name from a market then established though no enrolment of its charter has hitherto been discovered. Newmarket palace was originally built by James I, for the purpose of enjoying the amusement of hunting, and to this house was his unfortunate successor, Charles I, conveyed a prisoner by the Parliament, in 1647, where he remained about ten days. During the civil wars the house as well as racing had fallen into decay; but on the restoration both revived under the patronage of 'The Merry Monarch', who rebuilt the 'house' for his better accommodation, and hence it has the appellation of a Royal 'palace', The King making it his abode, and not only personally attending the races, but, according with John Evelyn, keeping and entertaining horses in his own name; and then the glory of Newmarket, so long obscured, again shone in meridian splendour.

18th May 1836   Bury & Norwich Post

NEWMARKET UNION To BUILDERS

The Board of Guardians of this Union, will at their meeting on Friday the 3rd of June next, receive tenders from any persons willing to Contract for the Erection of the New Central Workhouse. According to the design of Mr William Pardoe Root, Architect of Evershold Bedfordshire, and under his superintendence. William Parr Isaacson Newmarket 11th May 1836

11th June 1836

Yesterday Messers Steggles and Son, builders, of Bury, obtained the contract for erecting the New Union Workhouse, at Newmarket, and began the same on the following Monday, this is the third building of the above description now erecting by the above firm.

In about 1830 the Guardians of Newmarket Union of Parish Houses who were also responsible for the administration of the poor relief, decided at a meeting at Kingston House Newmarket that there was a need for a new workhouse. In 1836 they purchased 4 acres of land in Exning Road at an isolated spot outside the town. There were no houses between Bakers Row and the Union Workhouse and beyond there the next habitation was at Exning village. Around the same date Unions were built at Bury St Edmunds, Haverhill, Cambridge, Sudbury and Linton. Heasman.

William Steggles [1777-1859]. County Surveyor for West Suffolk. He was the son of William Steggles [1752-1834]. The father and son constituted a small building firm in the first half of the 19th C.

1837

11th March 1837

Died – On Monday last, aged 88, Charles Hammond, Esq., of the firm of Eaton, Hammond, and Son, bankers Newmarket. He was an excellent father, friend and neighbour, with a character composed of the brightest of Christian virtues was this esteemed man 'gathered to his fathers'.

Eaton Hammond & Son bankers were in the High Street now Barclays Bank. Pigots 1839

1840

29th February 1840

Newmarket Theatre. From a correspondent. We never remember to have experienced a greater theatrical treat than that which was provided for us on Thursday evening, the 20th instant by Mr Feist's unwearied exertions on the occasion of his annual benefit. The pieces selected were *The School of Reform* and *The Honey Moon* in the former of which Mr Rayner, who had volunteered his valuable assistance, represented his favourite part of *Tyke*. Mr Rayner has already gained so much celebrity in that character, that it would be superfluous to say that a highly respectable and crowded audience testified their enjoyment of his performance by the most enthusiastic plaudits. Mr Feist personated *Lord Avondale*, with his usual just conception of character. Mr Saker, of the Garrick Theatre, London, fully sustained his reputation in the character of *General Tarragan*; and Messrs Woodley and G Soar (amateurs, we believe) exhibited as the representatives of *Ferment* and *Frederick*, with considerable histrionic talent, and were deservedly applauded. Mr James Powell, from London, played the *Old Man*, with much feeling. Mrs Gomersal, of the Garrick Theatre, London, in the character of *Mrs Ferment*, and Mrs Feist as *Madam St Clair*, were perfectly 'au fait'. 'A young lady' made her first appearance as *Julia Tarragan*, and was well received; at the end of the play she danced a *Pas Seul* in first rate style, and, as *Zamora* in the 'Honey Moon' improved the favourable impression which she had made on the audience. Master F Feist in the song of 'Bobby Miles the Charity Boy', greatly amused; and was unanimously encored. Miss Feist as *Juliana*, in the 'Honey Moon' was greeted on her entrance with the most enthusiastic applause. Too much praise cannot be awarded her for her judicious and spirited representation of the character. Her modest, unaffected manner will ever render her an especial favourite with the public. Mrs Gomersal as *Violante*, delighted everybody by her tact and liveliness. Mr Feist, by his elegant and admirable performance of *The Duke*, fully justified the partiality of his friends. Mr Rayner's, *Mock Duke* was the very incarnation of burlesque dignity, and produced shouts of laughter. *Lampedo, Count Montalban, Rolando,* and *Balthazar,* found their impersonators in Messrs. Saker, Woodley, G Soar, J Powell, and the performance throughout was rewarded by the most gratifying manifestations of approbation. The orchestra was composed of members of the Newmarket Amateur Musical Society and of the Harmonic Band, who, with their usual good nature, tendered their efficient services, and played during the evening several highly popular pieces.

Robert Rayner, Boot and Shoe maker, on the Cambridge side of the High Street Newmarket Directory 1844. Charles Feist ran a boarding and day school in Back Lane. Pigots 1839

31st October 1840

The Bazaar – In addition to the races, this season, and a great deal of company has been attracted by the holding of a bazaar for the benefit of several charitable institutions. It commenced on Wednesday morning, at the Kingston-house, and as might be expected from the illustrious patronage bestowed on it, attracted visitors from all parts of surrounding counties; the rooms, in fact were crowded to excess, and a desire to possess the elegant lots exposed for sale was so good that the most extravagant prices were obtained. The Duchess of Beaufort, the Countesses of Albemarle and Chester, Lady Jermyn, Mrs Portman, and several other ladies proved themselves excellent shopkeepers; and it is gratifying to add that their benevolent exertions obtained a return unequal to their expectations, the sum of £517, being taken. On Thursday the rain fell in torrents the whole day, so the sum of £206 only was received. The ball in the evening was most brilliantly attended.

The newspaper that this report appeared in was so tightly bound that some of the words at the beginning of lines had to be added.

At this period it was fashionable for wealthy ladies to hold bazaars and act as shopkeepers, a novelty for women who were looked after hand, foot and finger by a bevy of servants. The first Bazaar of its kind in England was the Soho Bazaar in the north west corner of Soho Square, London. Started by John Trotter, as a depot for the sale of articles in aid of the widows and orphans of soldiers who fell in the Napoleonic war and to promote 'female and domestic industry'. Stalls could be hired by the day, and the goods sold were largely the sort of thing that women could produce at home – lace, jewellery, gloves, millinery and potted plants. It was opened by Queen Charlotte in 1816, and became most frequented by sightseers especially at Christmas, New Year's Day, and other gift seasons. It was extensively patronised by the royal family and the Princess of Russia honoured it in 1868. The business carried on until 1889.

1841

9th October 1841

The Revising Barristers commenced business at Newmarket on Tuesday morning, shortly after eleven o'clock, at the Rutland Arms, Mr Gurdon being sufficiently recovered to resume his duties. There was an absence of both political parties, and nothing further to do than to revise the overseers' lists, which, in a great number of instances, was attended with unnecessary trouble, as the overseers seem determined never to understand their duties. Mr Gurdon told one of the overseers, while censuring him for his stupidity, that the country was put to an extra expense of £20,000 per ann., by the overseers not attending to the instructions of the Act of Parliament; and yet nothing could be more simple. Hundreds of overseers left themselves open to penalties of £500, and had the law been altered, so that overseers could be punished by giving the Barristers power to inflict a small penalty – say £5 – instead of their being subject to a penalty of £500., he should feel sometimes bound to put it into force, and most unquestionably he would have done so in the present instance, as he had copied his list from a wrong copy, and inserted the names a fresh of persons who were last year struck off as dead, and he could not conceive a case of grosser inattention.

11th December 1841

The Newmarket coach, on its way to London, on last Friday week, was robbed of a carpet bag belonging to Mr Eaton, and containing, besides linen and apparel, £100 in bank notes, all new notes of Messrs. Gibson and Co.'s Saffron Walden Bank (in eight £10 notes, numbered 2,233 to 2,240, and four £5 notes). The carpet bag, which bore the owner's name, 'Richard Eaton, Esq., Newmarket.' Upon a brass plate, was afterwards found in Pond's Lane, near Clapton; from which, it appears the robbery had been committed in that neighbourhood. It had been broken open and rifled of all the valuable property, but a few articles of linen were left in it.

Richard Eaton Esq., Stetchworth House. Pigots 1839

1842

12th February 1842

On Thursday week, upon the occasion of the introduction of the eldest daughter of W Isaacson, Esq., to society, that gentleman gave entertainments to his friends of the most gratifying and pleasing character. They commenced with amateur dramatic perform-ances at the theatre, the pit of which was boarded over and carpeted, and the centre box removed, so forming an elegant saloon. The pieces selected were *Town and Country* and *The Honest Thieves*. These representations were far beyond what might have been conceived of amateur performances. After their determin-ation the immediate friends of Mr Isaacson attended by special invitation, a ball and entertainment at his private residence conducted on a most liberal scale, in which all present evidently felt they were partaking of a hearty welcome and liberality of English hospitality. There were upwards of two hundred ladies and gentlemen present, all of whom expressed but one feeling of satisfaction and delight at the whole proceedings.

William Parr Isaacson, Attorney, High Street, also Clerk to Magistrates, Clerk to Commissioners of Property & Income, Land & Assessed Taxes, & to Poor Law Union, & Superintendent Registrar. PO Directory 1847. In 1841 William Parr Isaacson, wrote a sporting play or Legend of the Turf entitled Alice, or the Rye House Plot. *Silzer*

6th August 1842

On Thursday, the 28th of July, the first anniversary of the re-opening of the Independent Chapel, Newmarket, was celebrated, when sermons were preached by the Rev. H L Adams, of Newark. In the afternoon a public meeting was held: after prayer offered by the Rev. F R Moore, of Soham, the cause of religion in the town and neighbourhood was earnestly pleaded by the Rev. H Coleman, of Wickhambrook, W Selbie, D Flower, J Hobson, H L Adams, and S B Johnson; after the meeting, about 140 friends retired to take tea, in the large room, Kingston House. A most delightful spirit of harmony and Christian affection pervaded the assembly; an extra subscription was suggested by the chairman (E. Ball, Esq.), who set a very liberal example, and the sum of £11 was cheerfully

contributed in addition to the collection of the day, for liquidating the debt upon the chapel.
The Independent Chapel was at the junction of Fitzroy Street and Black Bear Lane.
Stephen Piper, Esq., Kingston House (behind York Buildings, High Street). PO Directory 1847. Edward Ball Esq. lived in Burwell.

5th November 1842

On Saturday the Duke of Cambridge arrived at the Palace Newmarket, upon a visit to the Duke of Rutland. They attended Divine Service at both the parish churches, on Sunday, and on Monday had a splendid battue on the preserves of the Duke of Rutland, killing upwards 500 head of game. His Royal Highness returned to town on Wednesday.
Duke of Rutland, Cheveley Park. Pigots Directory 1830. See 10th November 1849.

5th November 1842

Newmarket Fair – Mr Batty intends to pay a visit to Newmarket fair; a large and commodious place is now building for his riding school. We hear that Wombwell's wild beasts are also en route for the same place. A greater number of shows, etc., are expected than have been here for many years past. – On Thursday afternoon, the citizens of London were somewhat amused by the procession of Mr Hylton's vans of trained animals, passing through Fleet Street, St Paul's Churchyard, and Cheapside, on their way from Windsor to Newmarket, one of the vans being drawn by a large Ceylon elephant, Mr Hylton himself walking by the elephant's head. The elephant was harnessed with a huge harness and traces, after the manner horses usually harnessed. It was singular to see the stupendous beast thrusting his trunk first on one side and then on the other, in search of and receiving fruit from the crowd that accompanied him, while he was pursuing his way apparently wholly unconscious of the burthen he was drawing.
Pigot's Directory 1830 lists two fairs in the year at Newmarket, Whit Tuesday and the 8th November the latter was very extensive for cattle, horses, corn, butter, cheese, hops etc. The Post Office Directory of 1847 lists Whit Tuesday for stock and Hollymas fair in November a pleasure fair famous for sausages.
George Wombwell, who kept a boot and shoe shop in Old Compton Street, London, between 1804 and 1810, having an entrepreneurial flair he started with two snakes bought at a knock-down price, this rapacious, dwarfish drunk

nevertheless managed to assemble three hugely successful menageries which travelled the length and breadth of England and made him a wealthy man by the time of his death in 1850. Soho Past

3rd December 1842

Coroner's Inquest – On Tuesday last, before Mr Waterman, gent, on the body of Mary the wife of Robert Horsley, tailor, of Newmarket, who expired suddenly, on Sunday evening last. Verdict Apoplexy.
Robert Horsley, Wellington Street. Newmarket Directory 1844, not in the 1847 PO Directory?

1843

28th January 1843

The Newmarket Wesleyan Sunday School teachers have recently, on their own responsibility, erected a new school room, 30 feet long, at a cost of £107. Amongst the donors are the following gentlemen – J J Gurney, Esq. of Norwich; Lord Henniker, MP; J J Bigsby, Esq., MD of Newark; Sir C H Vere, MP; R Foster, Esq., Saffron Walden; and H S Wadding, Esq., A considerable sum, however, remains unpaid, and towards its extinction Mr Henry Hassell, hatter, Newmarket, is authorised to receive donations.
On the south side of the town stood the Wesleyan Chapel built in 1841. Pigots 1830. Henry Hassell, listed under Hatters, and described as 'manufacturer' Market Place. Pigots 1839.

28th January 1843

On Tuesday week, at Moulton, near Newmarket the remains of Miss Wilson, aged 91, sister to the late rector, were carried, in accordance with an expressed wish in her will, from the hearse to the grave by eight of the oldest women in the parish – their united ages amounted to upwards of 480 years.

11th February 1843

On Friday evening last, Mr Page surgeon, delivered a lecture on anatomy, at Mr Swindell's school room, Mill-hill, to a numerous and very respectable audience. The company was highly delighted with the talent which Mr Page displayed on this occasion, and we are glad to hear that he is about to give his friends a second treat of the kind.

Frederick Page, surgeon, High Street. John Swindell, academy, Mill Hill. PO Directory 1847

10th February 1843

Sunday School Union – On Thursday last the Newmarket and village Sunday–school Union held their twenty–third anniversary, at the Independent Chapel, E Ball Esq., of Burwell, in the chair. A report of the proceedings of the past year was read, and the Rev H Coleman, of Wickhambrook; the Rev – Johnson. The Rev – Slater, of Fordham, Rev J Cope, and several other gentlemen addressed the meeting; after which tea was provided at the large room, Kingston House when upwards of 100 sat down to an excellent and pleasing repast. It is gratifying to find that the Union now contains nearly 400 children, who are taught by gratuitous teachers, to whom their advance has been means of instructing 10,000 poor children to read the holy scriptures.

Rev James Cope (independent) Sun Lane. 1844 Newmarket Directory

6th May 1843

Inquest – An inquest was held at the Star Inn, Newmarket, on Thursday last, before Mr Phillips, coroner, on view of the body of William Hase, hairdresser, who hanged himself by his handkerchief to the head of his bed, about 5 o'clock the previous day. The jury returned a verdict 'That the deceased hanged himself in a fit of insanity, produced by habitual drunkenness.'

The Star Inn was shown on John Chapman's map of 1787 and dates back to at least 1625, the hearth tax of 1674 records 20 hearths. William Hase was not listed in Pigots 1839 Directory. He may have arrived in 1840 as the 1841 census recorded William Hase aged 35, Paradise Row, hair dresser, and his wife Ann. From above it appears he only lived in Newmarket for three years.

20th May 1843

Lamentable Instance of Sudden Death – An inquest was held at Newmarket, on the 15th instant, before Harry Wayman, Esq., on view of the body of Elizabeth, the eldest daughter of Mr Philip Arber, of the White Lion inn, who died on Friday the 12th inst. On retiring to bed the night before, she was in her usual health and spirits; at 4 o'clock was seized with spasms; and at noon was a corpse. A *post mortem* examination was made

by Messrs Peck and Faircloth, and the jury returned a verdict that the deceased *Died by the Visitation of God.* Miss Arber was in her 21st year, and her death is deeply lamented.

James Robert Peck and Richard Faircloth both Surgeons of High Street. Pigots 1839.

29th July 1843

Sunday School Union – On Wednesday last the teachers of the above Union gave the children a dinner of roast beef and plum pudding, to celebrate the abandonment of the Educational clauses of Sir James Graham's Factory Bill. The Union consists of five schools, vis., Newmarket, Dullingham, Ashley, Saxon St, and Moulton; about five hundred sat down to dinner in a capacious booth, erected in Mr Hull's paddock, (which was kindly lent for the occasion); after dinner the Rev J Cope, of Newmarket, delivered a very appropriate address, and the children returned to their respective homes; after which about three hundred and fifty teachers and friends sat down to tea, and several very excellent addresses were delivered by Messrs Andrews, Witnall, Swindell, Cope, etc. It was pleasing to observe several very respectable persons of the Established Church mingling with the Dissenters on this occasion, and ready to lend a helping hand. The day was fine and every thing was conducted in a very pleasing manner.

Sir James Graham became Home Secretary in 1841 and presented a scheme to Parliament in 1843 as part of a larger factory bill, to provide compulsory education of children in factories. A schoolmaster was to be appointed by the Bishop and a school board consisting of a majority of Anglicans. The Non-Conformists created widespread agitation to the scheme, because of this and a lukewarm reception by the Anglican church. Graham withdrew the bill.

Henry Andrews draper listed in Wellington Street in the 1839 Pigots Directory and then in High Street in 1847, John Swindell Academy Mill Hill. PO Directory 1847

9th September 1843

Inquest – An inquest was held at the Star Inn, Newmarket, on Thursday last; before Charles Phillips, Esq., one of the coroners for the county, on view of the body of a new–born female child, found the previous night in a privy on the premises of Mr Henry Hall. The jury, after a lengthened investigation, returned a verdict That the said child was the bastard child of Mary Rule of Newmarket aforesaid, single woman, but whether the said child was born alive or dead, or how the said child came to her death, there was not sufficient evidence to satisfy the jury'. We understand that a warrant will be issued for the apprehension of the said Mary Rule, on the charge of concealing the birth of the child.

Henry Hall, animal and portrait painter, Mill Hill. Pigots 1839; by 1847 he was residing as Artist, High Street. PO Directory 1847

25th November 1843

Newmarket Bank – The bank of Mr Bryant of Newmarket suspended payment on Friday the 17th but it would seem by the resolution of an influential meeting, which will be found in an advertisement that there is no doubt of the solvency of the concern though the assets are not immediately available. The delay, however, will no doubt prove injurious to many small tradesmen. We hinted last week at the above stoppage, and are now glad to find that the matters are said to be better than had been led to fear.

Robert Bryant and Son, Bankers, High Street draws on Hanbury's, Taylor and Lloyd, London. Pigot 1839

16th December 1843

On Thursday, the 12th inst., the inhabitants of Newmarket were favoured with a very interesting display of the attainments made by the young gentlemen of Mr Swindell's academy. Their examination in orthography, syntax, and parsing of the Latin, French, and English languages, geography, mathematics, etc., was minute and severe, but we did not observe an error in any of the answers. At the conclusions, S Piper, Esq., moved a vote of thanks to the tutor of this academy, and the Rev. J Cope seconded the motion, speaking in terms of high commendation, both of the master and pupils. The resolution was carried by a large respectable assembly.

Stephen Piper, Kingston House. Pigots 1839. Rev James Cope, independent, Sun Lane. Newmarket Directory 1844

1844

20th January 1844

On the morning of Friday the 12th instant, about two o'clock, the dwelling ~ house of W Rayner, Esq., of Stradishall-place near Newmarket, was broken into, and the following articles stolen, viz., a silver tea-pot, nearly plain; four old-fashioned salt spoons; several teaspoons, part of them plain, and some marked 'W.A.R.;' several desert spoons, marked 'R.'; a silver fruit knife, a pair of silver sugar tongs, and other articles; a reward of £500 is offered for the apprehension of the offenders.

6th April 1844

Birth in a Mail Coach. On Saturday evening, a lady who had just arrived in London by railway from Folkestone, started for Norwich by that mail, which goes from the Belle Sauvage, Ludgatehill, and after travelling outside a few miles on the road, she complained of sudden illness. Fortunately, there was room in the coach for another passenger, and the coach-man, John Edes, good naturedly assisted her therein where there were three gentleman seated. The lady now appeared to have recovered, and all went on well until they arrived within about five miles of Newmarket, when certain painful ejaculations having escaped her lips, the gentlemen hailed the driver, who, on opening the door, to his surprise discovered that his four inside passengers had increased to five, the lady having given birth to a fine boy. On their arrival at Newmarket, she was taken out of the coach and placed in an apartment provided for her at the hotel, and she is now going on well. She is the wife of a gentleman named Anderton, residing at Norwich. – *Times*

Belle Sauvage, (Bell and Savage), was an old galleried coaching inn on Ludgate Hill, London. Renamed International Hotel in 1851 and pulled down in 1873. Charles Harper in his book The Newmarket, Bury, Thetford, and Cromer Road, *refers to the Norwich Mail via Newmarket and Bury, as being taken over by Robert Nelson of the Belle Sauvage from Benjamin Worthy Horne of the Golden Cross (an old inn that stood in the Strand near Charring Cross Station). Harper suggests that Nelson only just made it pay as the Post Office insisted that the coach go via Bury, which involved a longer route to Norwich.*

In 1845 Messrs Bottom and Co's (the White Hart Newmarket) tender for conveying mailbags between Cambridge, Newmarket and Bury St Edmunds was accepted. Originally the service was by coach but this was replaced by mail cart. Early in 1847 Charles Bottom applied to be released from that part of his contract between Bury and Newmarket. Charles Bottom received no payment for this service, his only remuneration being the exemption from paying tolls. With the opening of the railway between Ipswich and Bury he was soon working his coach at a heavy loss. At the same time Charles Bottom commenced conveying the Newmarket bag to and from Chesterford instead of Cambridge. Mr Bottom quit the Cambridge Newmarket service on 30th September 1847 two days after the opening of the Chesterford to Newmarket rail-way. As the expense of sending the day bag by this branch railway would amount to £7 a year more than the revenue derived from it, the day mail was discontinued. Muggleton. See Jan 1832.

THIS COACH from NORWICH to LONDON by Newmarket every Day Conveys 8 Insides 4 in Each Body & 6 Outsides in the most Pleasant And Agreeable Stile of any COACH yet offer'd to the Public it Travels 108 in 17 hours & half Including half an hour for Supper & the time Of Changeing Horses on the Different Stages the Above Vehicle Is At Present drove by a Coachman who has drove this & others for the Above PROPRIETORS upwards of 19 Years without Overturning Or Any Material Accident happening to any Passengers or Himself.

The 'Expedition' Newmarket and Norwich stage, about 1798

6th July 1844

School Anniversary – The third anniversary of the Wesleyan Sunday School of this place, will take place (to-morrow,) when sermons will be preached by the Rev Elisha Baily, of Ely, in the afternoon and evening; and in the evening also eight scholars will engage in a dialogue on "Solomon and the two mothers," extracted from a popular work recently published by Thomas Hirst, author of "The Music for the Church," etc., etc., This school was established on the 14th of March 1841, 205 children have been received, and 131 scholars (90 of whom do not attend day schools,) are now receiving instruction from 17 teachers, whose labours are perfectly gratuitous.

10th August 1844

Extraordinary Productiveness – A poor man named Wm Ray, residing in Grosvenor Yard, Newmarket, has a Suffolk sow reared by himself, which, from twelve successive litters, has produced 194 pigs, and in no instance has she reared less than 12.

23rd November 1844

Bryant's Bank – The holders of notes of the above firm will be pleased to know that they are now paying the second dividend of 10s in the pound making in the whole 20s in the pound, but without interest.

30th November 1844

Another Highway Robbery – On the same evening Mr Carter was robbed, Mr Stebbing woodman to the Duke of Kent, as he was returning from Newmarket to Cheveley, was stopped and robbed of £3. 10s and his watch, fortunately as he has been able to swear to two of the fellows and they are committed for trial.

21st December 1844

Melancholy Death from Burning – An inquest was held on Friday last, at the Grosvenor Arms Inn, Newmarket, before Harry Wayman Esq., coroner, on view of the body of Mary Powell, aged 70 years, pew-opener of St Mary, Newmarket, when it appeared the old woman, who was quite feeble, was left alone sitting by the fire, and on a neighbour going in was so burnt,

A view of Newmarket, 1844

that she died almost instantly. Verdict – *Accidental Death.*
See 8th August 1857

1845

18th January 1845

Clothes Club – This excellent institution, which owes its rise to the benevolent exertions of the Rev John Taylor, perpetual curate of the small parish of All Saints, has again afforded very seasonable relief to several poor families of the labouring class, who, by subscribing threepence per week, became entitled to a ticket which enables them to procure clothing to the amount of seventeen shillings, the four shillings extra being contributed from the fund raised by Mr Taylor among the upper class of his parishioners. It is to be hoped that the great parish will follow the example of the little parish for 'of great riches there is no real use, except it be in the distribution, the rest is but conceit (so saith Solomon): where much is there are many to consume it and what hath the owner but the sight of it with his eyes?'

15th February 1845

Inquest – An inquest was held at the Star Inn, Newmarket, on Monday, 10th inst., before Charles Phillips, Esq., Coroner, on view of the body of Matthew Challice, aged 64, who retired to bed

on the previous Saturday evening apparently in his usual state of health, and the next morning about six o'clock he was found a corpse. Mr Mosgrove, assistant to Mr Faircloth, surgeon, stated that the deceased died of disease of the heart. Verdict accordingly.

3rd May 1845

A daring robbery was committed here about 11 o'clock on Tuesday night, on the person of Mr Wiseman, sen. Although within a few yards of the Horse and Groom, he was stopped by three men, pulled of his horse, robbed of his watch and £10 in money, and brutally ill-treated. The ruffians made their escape before their victim was sufficiently recovered to give an alarm.

12th July 1845

The Theatre – Our old friend and much esteemed favourite Mr Gill, has, we hear, entered upon the lesseeship of this theatre. While we much regret Mr Gill's retirement from the well-deserved plaudits of Cambridge audience we sincerely wish him every success in his present undertaking.

18th October 1845

Accident – We are sorry to have to record an accident of a very serious nature, which befell the Rev John Taylor, minister of All Saints,

Newmarket, a few evenings ago. It appears that the Rev. gentleman was returning in his gig from Exning, when, at a sharp angle of the road, the night being very dark, the vehicle was run on to a bank, whereby Mr Taylor was thrown out, pitching on his head and receiving a concussion of the brain, with other severe injuries. He was shortly after taken up in an insensible state, and conveyed to his residence at Newmarket, where, we are glad to learn that, under very able medical treatment, he is likely to do well.

1st November 1845

Theatre news – Our old friend Mr Gill, who for the last 14 years has been attached to the Norwich circuit has become the lessee of the Newmarket and Woodbridge Theatres, and opens at the former place early in the present month. We heartily wish him success.

8th November 1845

Mr Gill's theatre opens on Monday night next, with *The Hypocrite* and *The Momentous Question*, two very capital pieces, and we hope Mr Gill's success will be commensurate with his skill and enterprise.

13th December 1845

Enormous Turnip – A white turnip, was taken up on Tuesday last, upon a field adjoining the Racing Heath, in the occupation of Messrs. C J and W Bottom, weighing upwards of 14 pounds, and measuring in circumference one yard and an inch; it may be seen at the shop of Mr Simpson, Bookseller, Market-place, Newmarket. (We have had several larger turnips brought to our office – one weighing upwards of sixteen pounds. Ed).

Allen Simpson, printer, bookseller, binder, stationer, newspaper agent and agent to London & Edinburgh Assurance Company, Market Place. PO Directory 1847. It was a Mr Simpson that founded The Newmarket Journal *later in the century.*

1846

26th March 1846

Awful Death – An inquest was held on Thursday, the 26th inst. at the Greyhound Inn, Newmarket, before Harry Wayman, Esq., coroner, on view of the body of Thomas Dyson, aged 25 years. It appears from the evidence that the deceased and a man by the name of Sydenham, a tailor, at Newmarket, went to Cambridge in a light cart, and on the road took up a young man by the name of Edward Craske, these three men stopped at the Butchers Arms, in Barnwell, and drank several quarts of beer, and had dinner; they then proceeded to Cambridge, and after visiting several public houses, partaking of beer and porter at each place, returned to the Butchers Arms, and had tea, but in the evening, just before starting, they had two half-pints of gin: the deceased drank all the first half-pint, but one glass, and one glass of the second half-pint, the deceased saying he could drink more than he (Sydenham) could pay for, and appeared to drink out of bravado, and got into the cart and laid at the bottom; they stopped at the Prince Albert, Quy, had some beer, and at Bottisham could not rouse the deceased, and when he was taken out of the cart at Newmarket, was dead. Mr S Gamble, surgeon, of Newmarket was sent for at half past ten o'clock, on Monday night, to see the deceased, just as he was brought home, his body was quite warm, but he was dead. Mr Gamble said in evidence, "I detected a strong smell of gin about him; I found no injury upon his person; his abdomen seemed to be distended, his mouth and tongue covered with a thick fur, the pupils of his eyes were dilated, his face pale and shrunken, and from the appearance he died of congestion of the brain, arising from excessive drinking of ardent spirits." In justice to Craske we must state he was quite sober, not having drank so much as Sydenham and deceased. The jury, after a short time, returned a verdict of 'Died from excessive drink,' and the coroner highly censured the conduct of Sydenham.

12th September 1846

No science appears to have made greater progress within the last few years than that of surgery. The truly unfortunate cases of distortions of the limbs and feet, the latter usually called club feet, are now cured by a slight surgical operation; where patients have been subjected for years to the painful method of treatment by mechanical distension, and this without success. We have just witnessed an extraordinary cure of this kind, operated upon by Mr Page, of Newmarket; and although only having been performed five weeks, the patient is perfectly cured, and able to walk. This patient was Mr Hitchcock's son, of Bridge Street Cambridge.

19th September 1846

Suicide of a youth under 16 years of age – On Tuesday last, an inquest was held at the Bull Inn, Newmarket, before H Wayman, Coroner, on view of the body of Charles Jarvis, second son of Mr Jarvis of the Greyhound Inn under 16 years of age, who was found hanging in a barn the previous day; no cause appeared for the rash act, and the jury returned a verdict of Temporary Insanity.

Bull Commercial Inn, Thomas Smith. High Street. William Jarvis, Greyhound Commercial Inn. High Street, PO Directory 1847. The Greyhound later became the Carlton Hotel.

3rd October 1846   CC

NEWMARKET AND CHESTERFORD RAILWAY
TURNING THE FIRST SOD

The formal commencement of the works upon the Newmarket and Chesterford Railway, popularly known as the "turning of the first sod," took place last Wednesday, in the parish of Dullingham, upon the property of the heir of the late General Jeaffreson, the eldest son of William Pigot, Esq. The spot selected was very near the public road, about a mile from Mr Pigot's residence, Dullingham Hall. A charming day attracted a large concourse of spectators; the village was alive with unwonted gaiety, and conveyances freighted with fair ladies, poured upon the scene of action in quick succession from the surrounding district. About 11 o'clock, the Directors and a large party of ladies and gentlemen left Dullingham Hall in procession, preceded by a band of music from Newmarket, a collection of handsome silk banners, and a body of 'navvies' apparently well-conducted men, who presented quite a respectable appearance in their clean white smock-frocks. Amongst the company in the procession we noticed Lord George Manners, MP (chairman), and Messers Fairlie, Hunt, Shelly, Tyrrell, and Fuller, Directors of the Company; W Pigot Esq., and his son, Master Jeaffreson, a fine youth about 10 years old; Sir Thomas and Lady Pigott; Captain and Mrs Tulloh; Mrs and Misses Benyon; Mr Tharp; Mr and Mrs Isaacson, and Mrs Fairlie; Revs Dr Banks, W Acton, etc.

Upon reaching the entrance to the field, Mr Jackson, the eminent contractor, took hold of the barrow, with the spade in it, and wheeled them at the head of the procession to the appointed spot It had been arranged that Master Jeaffreson should perform the ceremony of raising the first sod; accordingly the young gentleman divested of his coat, and stood, spade in hand, ready for his task. The young gentleman gave a few hearty digs into the earth, and having partially filled his barrow wheeled it along and tilted its contents, amid the cheers of the spectators... Active operations commenced on Thursday, and we understand that there will soon be from 2,700 to 3,000 men at work, in order to get the line into operation before the October meetings next year.

The railway line to Newmarket started as a branch line connecting to the main line that left the Eastern Counties Railway at a junction at Stratford, first to Broxbourne in 1840 and then to Bishop's Stortford in 1842. It was extending to Cambridge then Ely, connecting with the Norfolk Railway at Brandon and thence to Norwich in 1845. The Newmarket Chesterford Railway was incorporated in 1846 to construct a line of 16¼ miles from a junction at Great Chesterford to Newmarket. There was to be a 8¼ mile branch from Six Mile Bottom to Cambridge. The main line to Newmarket was opened on 3rd January 1848 for freight and from 4th April 1848 for passengers. Difficulties with finance forced the closure of the line from 30th June to 9th September 1850, reopening when a new board of directors were elected. The Cambridge branch was finally completed on 9th October 1851. The same day the Great Chesterford to Six Mile Bottom section closed and was finally dismantled in 1858.

7th November 1846

The Swell Mob – On Monday week, about eight o'clock in the evening, two men entered the shop of Mr Robert Hull, watchmaker and jeweller, and asked to look at some wedding rings. Mr Hull, thinking they looked rather suspicious characters, kept a sharp look out, while showing the property; the men, not being satisfied with the weight of the rings, were about leaving, when Mr Hull saw one of them attempting to conceal one, and charged him with the robbery. The other man slipped out of the shop, and, whilst Mr Hull was looking after him, the other slipped the ring back on the glass-case, but he was seized and detained until a policeman was found and took him into custody. He was taken the next day before the magistrates, and committed to Bury goal to take his trial, where he will have the pleasure of remaining for three months, as the sessions terminated the same day.

Robert Hull, watchmaker, High Street. PO Directory 1847

14th November 1846

Wholesale pig stealing - On Tuesday night six fat hogs and ten store pigs were stolen from the premises of Mr J Holmes, of Newmarket. The bold thieves have as yet saved their bacon; but we have little doubt but they will be heard off.
John Holmes, butcher, Mill Hill. PO Directory 1847

12th December 1846

On Sunday last, a fine-toned organ was opened at All Saints' Church, Newmarket, by the Rev J Gibson, M.A., rector of Worlington, Suffolk, who in a forcible and eloquent discourse, expatiated most fully on the beauty and antiquity of psalmody. The Rev. gentleman took for his text, the 5th chapter of 2nd Chronicles, 13-14 verses. The organ was played in a masterly style by Mr. J T Frye, organist, of Saffron Walden. A superior choir was in attendance. The collection was most liberal.

1847

23rd January 1847

Dreadful accident – On Friday the 15th instant, a man of the name of Collis, in the employ of C Phillips, Esq., Newmarket, was feeding a thrashing machine, and was in the act of getting down, when he fell, and his arm was drawn into the machine; when the break completely severed his hand, just above the wrist, and dreadfully lacerated the arm; so much so that amputation above the elbow, was necessary, but we are happy to hear he is as well as the case will admit of.
There were two C Phillips listed in Newmarket. Charles Phillips, attorney, Albion Street. Pigot 1830. Charles Phillips, brewer, Wellington Street. PO Directory 1847

20th February 1847

Irish Distress - We rejoice to say that there has been collected, by the Rev. John Taylor, incumbent of the small parish of All Saints, Newmarket, for the distressed Irish and Scotch, the sun of £31. 8s. 2d. This liberal collection surely will stimulate others, who have the care of small parishes, to use the like exertion.
The starvation and death of large numbers of Irish people 1847-51, following a blight that in 1845 ruined the potato crop, the staple diet of the population.

18th September 1847

On Thursday last, Mr Hughes's Mammoth Establishment entered this town in grand procession, but just before the first performance was to have commenced, the centre pole of the booth was broken by the violence of the wind, and down came the whole of the covering, which was very much shattered. Had this accident happened an hour later, we think, in all probability, the result might have been serious. No performance took place in consequence, to the great disappointment of many, especially to the "Country Cousins," several of who came from a distance.

16th October 1847

Provident Society, and Self Aiding Medical Club. – The general annual meeting of the members of this society, was held at Newmarket, on Tuesday week, his Grace the Duke of Rutland, K. G., President of the society, occupied the chair. The secretary read the report by which it appeared that during the past year, 4174 recipient members have enjoyed the advantages and privileges of the medical club, and have contributed £233 towards providing themselves with medical attendance; 168 poor women have also, through this society, obtained the skilful assistance in their confinements of the medical practitioner of their own choice. A vote of thanks having been passed upon the noble chairman, he addressed the society upon the success and usefulness of such an institution. Other resolutions were also moved, and votes of thanks passed to various officers.

1848

3rd June 1848

We are glad to find that it has been at length determined to abolish the dangerous and inconvenient custom of exposing cattle for sale in the public streets of this town. On the 23rd ult., at a meeting of the agriculturists, cattle dealers, and others, held at Newmarket, resolutions were passed (which we advertised last week) condemnatory of the practice; and declaring that the practice had been abolished in other towns, not only without detriment to those markets, but with an accession of considerable improvement.

Was this the time when the cattle market was moved behind the Waggon and Horses inn, where the Rookery car park is now?

24th June 1848

Classical and Commercial Academy. – On Monday the 12th inst., the annual examination of pupils of Mr Swindell took place, in the presence of several clergymen and a highly respectable company of ladies and gentlemen. The young gentlemen were examined in Greek, Latin, French, Natural Philosophy, History, Geography, Astronomy, English Grammar and Recitation, with some other branches of learning, the subjects of their studies during the session. The whole was conducted to the highest satisfaction of the judges, who had been specially invited to witness the mode of teaching and its successful result. As a testimony of this satisfaction, the following judges of the examination most cordially subscribed their names: - Edmund Mirtlock, BD, Rector of Moulton; James Davies, Haverhill; W Cantlow, Isleham; D Flower, Burwell; J Richardson, Barton Mills; J P Simpson, Newmarket; J Pilgrim, Hitcham.

29th July 1848

Serious Loss – On the morning of Thursday last Mr J Holmes, butcher, of Newmarket whilst walking from his residence on the Mill Hill, to his shop on the Market place, had the misfortune to lose his pocket book, containing checks (*sic*) and notes to a considerable amount, the former of which are stopped payment, but we regret to say Mr Holmes will probably sustain a loss exceeding £50, as hitherto no tidings have been heard of his serious loss.
John Holmes, butcher, Mill Hill. PO Directory 1847

11th November 1848

Highway Robbery – On Saturday evening week, as Mr Deeks, of the Victoria Inn, Newmarket, was returning from Cambridge at about seven o'clock, when within three miles of home (a lonely spot) he was stopped by three ruffians, who knocked him off his horse, gagged him, and robbed him of all the money he had about him, amounting to 7s 6d. Happily he did not carry with him the sum he had intended, or he would, no doubt, have lost the whole.
Francis Jas. Deeks, Victoria and wheelwright, Exning Road. PO Directory 1847

11th November 1848

Violent Assault – Wednesday last being fair day, a great number of people were attracted to the town; amongst the rest were a gang that appear in our police report of Monday. One of these, who gave his name Elisha Brown, better known to the police of Cambridge as Cranky Jack, offered to buy a horse off a farmer. The price was settled and demanded, but Cranky said he should like to see the horse go through his paces, and wished to mount him; no doubt with the intention of testing his lasting qualities, by seeing how far he would go without stopping. The farmer, however, would not part with his nag until the needful was forth coming; whereupon Cranky dealt him a severe blow with a stick which brought him to the ground, and for a time rendered him insensible. He immediately took to his heels across the fields towards Dullingham and several farmers, who were mounted, attempted to follow, but were prevented by the rest of the gang, who took hold of the horses heads to prevent their pal being pursued. The foot passengers, however, followed, and after a short burst headed and captured him. On Thursday he was taken before a magistrate and fully committed for trial. The Attorney-General to this class of individuals was in attendance directly after capture, but could not find any of his clients, who had no doubt caught sight of the well-known features of Inspector Jaggard, who was on the look-out for them, and had decamped.

25th November 1848

Sheep Stealing – This offence appears to be greatly on the increase in the neighbour hood of Newmarket, as, in addition to one stolen from Edward Gardner, and one stolen a short time since from Mr Sabin, the skin and entrails of another belonging to Mr Staples, of Moulton, were found on Friday morning week, in a plantation between Newmarket and Ashley; and on the same day the remains of part of another, from which the flesh had been cut, were found in a field in the parish of Cheveley.

16th December 1848

The Theatre – During the last week, under the able management of Mr Charles Gill, has been a scene of great attraction, as Mrs Gill and Mr Clark Fisher have been starring it in several of their favourite pieces. Mr Fisher is a well-known favourite at Newmarket, Mrs Charles Gill is known everywhere.

1849

13th January 1849

Harmonic Society – On Thursday 11th instant, the Members of the above Society celebrated their fifteenth anniversary, at the Five Bells Inn; on which occasion, twenty-nine sat down to a sumptuous dinner, provided by host R Moody Hassall; after the cloth was removed, several loyal toasts were given; and during the evening the company were enlivened with some very excellent songs. The chair was ably filled by Mr J Daley, and the vice-chair by Mr Moody. The company separated at a late hour, highly delighted with the day's enjoyment.

Five Bells, Robert Hassall, Mill Hill. John Daley, horse trainer, Jockey Lane. PO Directory 1847

10th February 1849

Ancient Shepherdry – On Monday, the 5th inst., the members of the 'Shepherds on the Turf Lodge' celebrated their second anniversary at the White Lion Inn, Newmarket, when 45 sat down to a most excellent dinner, provided by brother Philip Arber; after the cloth was removed, several loyal toasts were given. The chair was ably filled by brother Charles Clarke. The company separated at a late hour, highly delighted with the evening's amusement.

Philip Arber, White Lion, & stone mason, High Street. PO Directory 1847. The Arbers were a Burwell family and owned clunch pits there. Clunch is a light chalk stone and was used in many of the local fen edge village buildings and also for some of the delicate carving found in Ely cathedral.

24th February 1849

Fire – On Saturday, about twelve o'clock noon, a fire broke out upon the premises of Mr Robert Bocock, grocer and cheesemonger, situate in Wellington Lane, which, at first threatened to be of a most alarming and destructive character, but which was, fortunately, soon extinguished, by the timely arrival of an engine, the quick and plentiful supply of water from the reservoirs belonging to the brewery of Charles Phillips, Esq., and the praiseworthy assistance of the neighbours and inhabitants of the town. The flames were entirely confined to the cellar under the shop, which contained a portion of Mr Bocock's stock in trade, consisting chiefly of soap, candles, tobacco, etc. From evidence which has since been collected by Mr E Feist, the resident Fire Agent, with respect to the origin of the fire, it appears that one of the shop boys went into the cellar between nine and ten o'clock in the morning; that he then accidentally broke a carboy containing a small quantity of spirits of turpentine, which escaped over the cellar floor; that he collected a portion of it, and returned to the shop; that, after, some time had elapsed, he went again into the cellar with a lighted candle, to gather up the other portion of the spilt turpentine, when the candle either dropped from his hands into the turpentine, or the fumes of the spirits coming into collision with the lighted candle, instantly ignited, and communicated its destructive powers to the stock in the cellar. We are informed that the whole of Mr Bocock's property is insured in the Imperial Fire Office, whose resident agent was on the spot within five minutes after the alarm was given. A serious amount of property has thus been fortunately preserved from conflagration; and as a caution to those persons who are ignorant of the fact, we beg to impress upon their minds that the fumes of turpentine, which is of a purely volatile character, will ignite from collision with any substance, in precisely the same manner as when a light is applied to gas.

Charles Phillips, brewer, Wellington Street. Ebenezer Feist, auctioneer and estate agent, High Street. PO Directory 1847
Robert Bocock, grocer, Wellington Street. Whites, 1855

14th July 1849

Melancholy Death by Burning – On Tuesday last, whilst Julia, the eldest daughter of Mr Marson, trainer, of Newmarket, was attending to some preserves over the fire, her dress, which was of muslin, ignited, and she was so dreadfully burned that she died the same evening. Her mother twice attempted to extinguish the flames by wrapping a rug around the deceased, but she threw it off, and rushed to the door. If she had had the presence of mind to throw herself upon the ground, the flames would have ascended from her, and might have been easily extinguished, without having occasioned much injury. The deceased was 21 years of age, and possessed such amiable qualities as endeared her to a large circle of relations and friends. –

Another account says:- Mrs Marson was superintending the making of some preserves, when Miss Marson, who was going out, entered the kitchen to speak to her mother. She went close to the fire, and having on a muslin dress it is supposed a gush of air carried it near the bars. In one instant she was a sheet of fire. Mr Marson ran down from his bedroom on hearing the dreadful screams, and Mr Blyth, who had just left the house, and was not more than a hundred yards off, hearing the cries, returned, caught the poor girl in his arms, put her on the ground, and extinguished the remaining flames, but scarcely a vestige was seen of her clothing. Surgical assistance was immediately sent for, and the lady put to bed. On removing the ashes that adhered to her, it was discovered that the only part on which any skin remained on the body was where the stays had protected it, the remainder was one mass of burned flesh. The most extraordinary circumstances is that the body is not deeply burnt in one part; the surface merely is scorched. Mr Marson, her father, is the highly respected trainer of that name.

Charles Marson, horse trainer, Terrace. PO Directory 1847

28th July 1849

An Unparalleled Example in the History of Wheat Growing - There is now growing in the garden of the Newmarket Union Workhouse the produce of two grains of wheat, planted by Mr E Clarke, the Master, upon the first of September, 1848, in two pots, and allowed to remain until the middle of November, when they were taken up, and the plants each separately divided; six sets were thus procured; these were planted in the natural soil, and allowed to remain until the middle of February, 1849, (being occasionally stopped during that period); they were again taken up, and each plant separately divided, whereby thirty six sets were procured; these were again planted in the natural soil, and the amazing proofs of its productiveness can be witnesses, as one grain has produced the extraordinary number of 164 ears, and the other 153 ears, and at least nine-tenths of them of unusually large size, covering twelve square feet of ground abundantly, five feet high.

20th October 1849

Last week, a butcher, at Newmarket named Chapman committed suicide, in his shop, by hanging himself. A coroner's jury decided that, at the time he committed the act, he was labouring under insanity.

Thomas Chapman, butcher. Market Place. PO Directory 1847

10th November 1849

The Fair – This fair was held on Thursday last, and was, in general, exceedingly well supplied with most descriptions of stock. The attendance of farmers and dealers was large, and though business was very dull in the early part of the day, owing to those who came to purchase standing out for lower prices. The difference was eventually adjusted, and large numbers, both of beasts and sheep. Were disposed of before the close of the day; but at prices rather lower than those which have prevailed at the late fairs in this town. Of beasts the show was rather good, the greater portion of which was disposed of. Of sheep the supply was very large. The show of horses was not large, but there were a few good cart horses. Some cart foals sold at rather high prices, some of which fetched from £16 to £18; of nag horses but a middling display. A great portion of stock left the fair unsold. Trade was described by the large dealers as very dull and heavy.

10th November 1849

Shooting - On Wednesday week, his Royal Highness the Duke of Cambridge arrived at the Palace, Newmarket, on a visit to his Grace the Duke of Rutland, and on Thursday and Friday his Royal Highness enjoyed some excellent shooting in his Grace's preserves. His Royal Highness left the Palace for London on Saturday last. On Monday last, his Grace the Duke of Rutland, Lord G Manners, MP, Colonel Anson, and J Fairlie, Esq., shot in Cheveley Park preserves and killed 200 pheasants, 104 brace of partridges, 50 hares, and four rabbits.

The 1st Duke of Cambridge, Prince Adolphus of Great Britain and Ireland, was born in 1774 in London and created Duke of Cambridge in 1801, he died in 1850. This report probably refers to the 2nd Duke, George William Frederick Charles, born March 1819 at Cambridge House, Hanover and became a colonel in the British Army in 1837.

Colonel George Anson, [1797-1857] MP was elected for South Staffordshire in 1818, married in 1830 to Isabelle, daughter of the first Lord Forester. He served in India and became Commander in Chief in India and died of cholera at Karrial India in 1857. Colonel Anson, High Street PO Directory 1847

1st December 1849

Turnip Show – We are requested to contradict a statement made in the *Cambridge Chronicle* last week, that the late Turnip Show, between Mr Smith, the landlord of the Bell Inn, at Newmarket, and Mr Goodchild of Cheveley. Mr Goodchild won the wager, and that it was the seventh year of his being the winner. This is not the fact. There have been 6 shows, and now each party has won 3 times. On this last occasion, Mr Goodchild produced 15 turnips, which measured three bushels.

15th December 1849

About 5 o'clock on Friday week a fire broke out in one of the old wings of the mansion at Upper Hare Park, the seat of Field Marshall Grosvenor, who, with the family, is now from home, the only persons residing there being a man servant and some females who are left in charge of the house. The servants were at tea at the time of the out break, when fancying they smelt fire the man ran up stairs and found the building was in flames. A dispatch was immediately sent to Newmarket for the engine, which was on the spot as soon as time would permit, but no person was there except the inmates of the house to assist in working it. The Messrs Bryant, Webster, Jacobs, and others who accompanied the engine, set to work in good earnest, and succeeded in confining the fire to that portion of the house in which it commenced, and which was entirely destroyed. The rest of the buildings, and all the new part of the mansion, was fortunately preserved. The fire is supposed to have been caused by the overheating of one of the flues, by which means some of the other wood-work became ignited.
Field Marshall, The Rt. Hon Thomas Grosvenor P C of the 65th Foot. He was the elderly cousin to Robert Earl Grosvenor, son of Richard Grosvenor, first Earl Grosvenor.

1850

23rd March 1850

Run-away Bankrupt – Richard Leach of Newmarket, tailor, should have gone up to the Bankruptcy Court on Monday, for the purpose of passing his last examination. The fiat was issued in the 18th of Jan. last, by Mr Edward Bonfellow, of Bury St, Edmund's linen draper, and on the 11th of February, Mr James Butcher, of Soham, linen draper, was appointed trade assignee. The bankrupt's debts are not known, as he has absconded with another man's wife, deserting his own family. The value of the stock, furniture, etc., seized by the messenger is about £220, and as the bankrupt did not appear, he was proclaimed an outlaw at the rising of the Court.
Richard Leach, tailor, Wellington Street. PO Directory 1847. James Butcher, Churchgate Street, Soham. Pigot 1830

27th April 1850

A thunderstorm, accompanied by a heavy fall of rain and hail, broke over this neighbourhood on Saturday afternoon. The peals of thunder, which, were extremely loud, followed each other in quick succession; the lightning was very vivid, and of a blue colour. A water spout was seen in the direction of Woodditton and Stetchworth. When first seen it appeared in the shape of a large speaking trumpet, the wider end being in the clouds. It afterwards assumed a horizontal position, and then disappeared. This was succeeded by a severe shower of very large hailstones.

18th May 1850

Child found in a well – This town has been thrown into a state of great excitement, in consequence of the body of a newly-born male child having been found in a well, on Wednesday, the 8th instant. It appears that the water in this well, proverbial for its purity and clearness, had of late become so foetid as to be quite unfit for domestic purposes, and many who had used it in kneading their dough, had perceived a nauseous taste and smell, and had even found portions of hair in their bread; but the cause was unknown till the day in question, when a person who had been drawing at the well, found a quantity of skin and hair in the bucket of water, and which eventually proved to be the scalp off a child; and on looking into the well saw something floating on the surface of the water. He immediately got a cinder sieve, and on drawing it up found the body of a male child, apparently about a month old. An inquest was held on the following day, at the Railway Tavern, before C Phillips, Esq.. Messers Fyson and Gamble made a post mortem examination of the body, and were of the opinion that the child was born alive, but were unable to swear positively, on account of the advanced state of decomposition, it being supposed that the body had been in the water upward of six or eight weeks. Several women were questioned relative to the pregnancy of a suspected person, but nothing of any material consequence could be come at. The Jury returned a verdict of –"Found in a well, but how or by whom it came there, there was insufficient evidence to prove." The strictest investigation is being made and it is to be hoped that the guilty party will soon be brought to justice.

The Railway Tavern, renamed The Carpenters Arms, is in Station Road, renamed All Saints Road. Robert Fyson, surgeon, High Street. Pigot 1839

8th June 1850

Newmarket Archaeological Institute The approaching meeting of the society at Newmarket is anticipated with much interest, and will probably be very numerously attended. Mr Deck, chemist of Cambridge, intends to contribute to the exhibition a number of specimens of Cambridge antiquities, amongst which will be a rare relic recently found at Wilbraham.

15th June 1850

Bury and West Suffolk Archaeological Institute ~ A meeting of this Society was held at the rooms, Newmarket, on Thursday, the 13th inst., and was well attended by many noted antiquarians. The members and friends of the Society made an excursion from Bury St Edmund's, through Gazeley, Moulton, Ashley, Cheveley, Wood Ditton, and other villages to Newmarket, for the purpose of inspecting several objects of antiquity and interest previously prepared for them. About 12 o'clock the party arrived at Cheveley Park, where their number was much increased by previous arrivals and resident friends and patrons. The first object of interest was the ruins and remains of the old castle, now an extensive plantation, but, without doubt, formally an isolated and important building, surrounded by a wide and deep moat, and approached by a draw bridge. The diameter of the building was about 80 or 90 yards. The remains now consist of two or three massive buttresses of stone work, partly enveloped in thick ivy. Upon one of these buttresses stands the trunk of a large oak tree quite hollow; a sufficient demonstration of antiquity. During the excavations, kindly facilitated by John Fairlie Esq., of Cheveley Park, a very large well was discovered, which is now being cleaned out. In this well several pieces of masonry were dug up, each bearing some antique figure, with the escutcheons of some very ancient family. The members then proceeded to the parish church where several objects of interest were exhibited. Some very perfect Norman arches still remain, and which, it is supposed, were used as repositories for the dead, or as the recesses for recumbent figures. In the north aisle a small recess, formally used as an almonry, a very curious niche, termed a pisino (piscina), and many other objects of ancient design were discovered. Every courtesy was shown, and information given to the members of the Society by the Rev. J T Bennet, the rector, and J. Fairlie, Esq., under whose exertions and directions the alterations and discoveries have been made. The party then departed to Newmarket, where a dinner was prepared for them and a large collection of articles of archaeological and general interest were displayed.

Cheveley Castle – John Pulteney had permission to crenellate his house in 1341 – the castle occupied an isolated moated site 750m north-west of the church and well away from the village. Traces survive of a curtain wall with circular towers and a gatehouse on the north side.

29th June 1850

Robbery by a Servant ~ A young girl named Mary Spinks, aged 15, servant to Mr Vince, draper, etc, York Buildings, Newmarket, has for some time past contrived to extract various articles of drapery from the shop of her employer, and appropriate them to her own use. Her recent conduct had excited the suspicions of Mr Vince, and a few days since she was observed with a rather valuable brooch upon her neck. Upon being questioned as to how she came possessed of it, she prevaricated for some time, but afterwards said that she had found it in some rubbish. Her boxes were then searched, and several shawls, stockings, gloves, and various other articles to the value of upwards of £12 were found secreted in them. She was immediately given into custody, and taken before the Rev. Jas. Thos. Bennet, at Mr Isaacson's office, and fully committed to Cambridge goal for trial.

York Buildings, built in 1832, stands between Kingston Passage and the Jockey Club in the High Street. Mr Vince was still in occupation at the time of the 1861 census, where it is recorded

William Vince (39) outfitter and draper with his wife Annie Vince (25) and sons Louis (5), William (3), and Bryan (11 months). Going back to the 1841 census the occupants of York Building was listed as Arabella Derisley aged 25, milliner and Mary Derisley aged 20 milliner and also Henry Andrews aged 40 draper, and James Houghton aged 25 draper. After William Vince the building was occupied by Henry Bullman in the late 19th C and then Ashfords and now Palmers. It appears that this shop has had connections with the drapery trade for 160 years, as it is still trading in this merchandise today.

13th July 1850

Rural Sports - The pleasure fair of this town has been greatly improved within the last three or four years, and is patronised by several gentlemen and families of distinction of the town and neighbourhood, who very kindly contribute towards a fund for the purpose of entertaining the public with a variety of rural sports and diversions. It was held on the Heath on Friday, the 5th, having been unavoidably postponed, Whitsun week being the accustomed time. The programme for the day was fraught with every thing of fun and frolic, tending to excite the risibility of the most serious, while nothing was offered to offend the most fastidious. Chief of the sports consisted of donkey, foot, and hurdle races, for various sums, from 7s 6d to upwards of £1; jingling and rolling matches, jumping in sacks, climbing well soaped scaffold poles, bobbing for oranges, and many other rustic games, which were kept up till late in the evening. During the afternoon there were two distributions of plum-buns to boys and girls, also to the children of the Newmarket Union. Several temporary stands, decorated with ever-greens, were erected with other accommodations for the ladies and respectable families of the neighbourhood, who attended in vast numbers. The day's diversions were greatly enhanced by the melodious strains of the Newmarket band, which voluntarily attended.

13th July 1850   C C.

Stealing spectacles at Newmarket, Jan Edwards (28) wife of John, described of no settled residence, charged with stealing at Newmarket a pair of silver spectacles the property of Henry Hull. Pleaded guilty, 14 days imprisonment.
Embezzlement at Newmarket William Death (39) charged with embezzling 5s 5d the property

of his master William Vince of Newmarket draper. Pleaded guilty, to be whipped.

10th August 1850

Pedestrianism – The mile foot race between Mole, the Newmarket Pet, and Nickoldson, the Running Butcher, two noted pedestrians, for £2 a side came off on the Cambridge Road, near the White Lion Inn, on Monday last. This race, and the celebrity of the men as runners, had created considerable interest among the sporting gents of this town and neighbourhood for some time previous, and was witnessed by a great number of respectable persons of both sexes. Mole was a slight favourite, at about 6 to 4, which was freely taken by the butcher's party. The time fixed for the spin was between one and two o'clock, when both men appeared in excellent condition, and anxious for the victory. After tossing for the choice of sides, they were off at a rattling pace, and ran side by side for the first quarter of the mile, which was gone over in less than one minute; the half mile was run in a few seconds under two minutes, when Mole took the lead and maintained it throughout, and eventually ran in an easy winner, by at least 100 yards. The winner performed the mile in 4 minutes and 34 seconds, and the other in 4 minutes and 50 seconds.

14th September 1850

The Market – For some time there has been a growing dislike to the continuance of the Market in the street of Newmarket, owing to the inconvenience arising to carriages. On Tuesday week, P.C. Steggles ordered Mr Preston, the cattle dealer, to remove his beasts, and afterwards threatened to take him into custody, on his refusal, Subsequently he came up to him again, and took him into custody. At the Petty Sessions last Tuesday, Steggles charged Mr Preston with assaulting him by holding up his stick at him. On this occasion, Mr Preston appeared by Mr Naylor, as his counsel; and, after the examination of a great many witnesses, the Magistrates dismissed the case. The question involves the right of the public to use the street of Newmarket for the purpose of a market, and will probably furnish some business for the lawyers.
The market days are Tuesday and Saturday the former for corn and vegetables, and the latter for articles of general consumption. Pigot 1830. On John Chapman's map of 1787 the market area in the old Rookery had been built up, leaving only a small market square next to the Bull Inn, so

presumably the market stalls had moved back into the High Street.

26th October 1850

A Suspicious Stranger – On Wednesday evening, the 2nd instant, being meeting week, a gentlemanly attired stranger was observed to be lurking about this town in a very suspicious manner, and attracted the notice of several by interrogating them about different inns and lodging houses. Between four and five o'clock the next morning, he was seen to be prowling about the streets, and it is stated that the front doors of two or three houses were heard to be tried about that time. He was seen to go towards the Rutland Arms where he entered some of the gentleman's sleeping apartments, with no doubt, the design of plundering; but, fortunately, the gentlemen were awoke by his entering; and upon being questioned as to what he did there, replied in the French language, that he had merely made a mistake. One of the gentlemen immediately jumped out of bed after him, so that he was obliged to make a hasty exit. Mr Sabine, the landlord, saw him enter and go up-stairs, but, thinking he was one of the gentlemen just going to bed, took no further notice of him. He afterwards made another mistake, by entering the bed-room of Mr Westley, of the Golden Lion Inn, but was again frustrated in his design, by being spoken to by Mr Westley, who happened to be awake at the moment. He next fell into another wilful hallucination, by going up to the White Hart, where he proceeded to enter what apartments he could, in the same manner he had done at the Rutland Arms. He left the town the same morning by the eight o'clock up-train for London. It was afterwards reported that a ten pound note was lost from one of the rooms at the White Hart.

Mr Flatman, the celebrated jockey of this town, while at Doncaster, was robbed of two coats by one of those dextrous thieves who attended the race course and other places of public amusement for the purpose of peculation. It appears that Mr Flatman had just returned from the course, and having occasion to leave his room for a short period, found, on again entering it, that some one had been in and stolen his two coats.

Ralph Westley, Golden Lion, High Street. PO Directory 1847
Nat Flatman, son of a farmer born in 1810 at Holton St Mary Suffolk. His first mount was Lord Exeter's Golden Pin in 1829 and his last was Duke of Bedford's Golden Pipin in 1859.

Known to be honest, sober, discreet and plain living, he received a bad fall in 1859 and died in 1860. He was buried under the tower of All Saints Church.

2nd November 1850

Important Sale – All the rich and costly furniture, and effects, of W P Isaacson, Esq., took place at his mansion, in this town, on Monday, the 21st instant, and the four following days. The magnificence of the property attracted a great number of gentlemen and connoisseurs from all parts of the country. In consequence of a number of Jews and brokers, from London and other large towns, being present on each day of the sale, a very spirited and exciting competition was maintained, especially on the fourth day, when all the splendid drawing-room furniture, the collection of pictures, and the rare Dresden, Sevres, Chelsea, and Oriental China, were disposed of. The 1st, 2nd, and 3rd days were devoted to the breakfast-room, study, dining-room, music-room, library furniture, glass, china, and earthenware, various bed rooms, and servants departments, etc. The fourth as stated above. The fifth to the library of books, and the cellars of wine. The rich china and drawing room furniture realised extraordinary prices; the following is a correct statement of several of the drawing-room lots:- A pair of china vases with raised flowers cupids and flowers, £37; four old Dresden vases, representing the four seasons £21; pair of salt cellars, supported by male and female figures, £12 10s; pair Dresden figures of Mars and Minerva, £27; mantel time piece £13 15s; china basin and ewer, £15; Sevres coffee cup and saucer, £15 15s.; a small antique tortoise-shell tray, richly inlaid with gold, with 2 ink-stands, taper-stand, bell, and pounce-box (formerly the property of Queen Charlotte), £63; Brussels carpet, £15 10s.; Brocade satin damask curtains to four windows, £20; two splendid chiffoniers, £42; two card tables, £10 5s; the two magnificent console glasses, in rich and massive carved and gilt frames, £152 5s; two indulging chairs, £12; chimney glass, £35 14s.; smaller glasses, £31; a splendid old Buhl and tortoise shell writing table, £41; two ebony cabinets, £28; with various other magnificent lots, too numerous to state, amounting to £982 8s The cellars of wine realised very high figures; several bins of full-flavoured old port sold at from £7 10s to £9 10s per doz., twenty dozen of which fetched £167 14s; the whole cellar amounting to £783. The whole of the effects, it is supposed, realised between

£4000 and £5000. Judging from public opinion too high an eulogium cannot be passed upon Mr Richard Tattersall, who from the admirable manner in which he conducted the sale, merited the approbation of all who heard him.

In the 1861 census William Isaacson, aged 84, was living with his son William Isaacson, aged 61, in the High Street, and at that date both widowers. The above may refer to a house belonging to William senior who sold up and moved in with his son.

16th November 1850

Robberies – An unparalleled number of robberies and depredations have been committed in this town during the fair. On Monday the constables and policemen were actively engaged in bringing up a great number of thieves and vagabonds, and the magistrates rooms were thronged. A man named Harwood was met by two desperate fellows and a woman near the Three Tuns Inn, between eight and nine o'clock on Monday morning, who turned his coat over his head, picked his pockets of all his money, and then knocked him down. They were afterwards apprehended, and taken before the magistrates, and fully committed to Cambridge for trial. The house of Mr Bocock, in Wellington lane was, feloniously entered by some thief or thieves who effected an entrance at the chamber window and escaped unobserved, with a sum of money. Another was found in the house of a Mr Jeffery, and has been apprehended. A party of thieves were secured and confined in the cage, but during the night their companions managed to take a portion of the roof off, but, fortunately, it happened to be the wrong side of the cage, which is divided into two separate apartments. Great praise is due to the constables for their indefatigable exertions.

Three Tuns Inn, James Clark, Market Place. PO Directory 1847

16th November 1850

Burglary – During the night of Wednesday last the shop of Mr Taylor, tailor, etc., near the Three Tuns Inn, was burglariously entered by some person or persons as yet unknown, and a quantity of cloth, etc., indeed very nearly all his stock in trade, to the value of £80. Stolen therefrom, Mr Taylor had been sleeping in the shop every night for the last week, as a protection to his property during the fair, till the night in question, when considering the premises safe he went home at his usual time. Of this, no doubt the thieves were appraised, who at once took advantage of the first opportunity.

Henry Taylor, tailor. Market Place. PO Directory 1847 & Whites, 1855

16th November 1850

Inquest – On Tuesday last an inquest was held at the Union Workhouse, Newmarket, before H Wayman, coroner, on the body of James Betts, a labourer, of Snailwell, aged 24 years. It appeared that the deceased and his wife came from Snailwell, on Saturday last, to Newmarket fair, to spend the anniversary of their wedding day, and on leaving the fair, about seven o'clock in the evening, to go home, had proceeded as far as the Crown Inn, in the High Street, when some girl caught hold of the deceased, supposed to be a girl of the town, and being repulsed by the wife, some man struck her, and the deceased interfered, but was struck down by an unknown hand; he was taken up insensible, carried to Mr Fyson's surgery, and died in a few minutes; the parties made off, and no one knows who the offenders were, nor has any suspicion. Verdict, 'Manslaughter, against some person or persons unknown.'

See 27th March 1852

14th December 1850

Effigies of the Pope and Cardinal Wiseman – (We have received the following statement from a correspondent, and insert it to show to what length the furore against Popery will carry persons, but totally disagree with the propriety of this and similar exhibitions. Editor). Friday week was a gala day in this town, in consequence of the Anti-Papistical and virulent feeling of the town and its environs being stimulated to make 'Guy Fawkeses' of the Pope and Cardinal Wiseman, whose effigies were exhibited, and finally consigned to the flames. During the week two gigantic figures representing the Pope and the Cardinal, attired in their canonicals, the former holding a crook and the latter a cross, were exhibited upon the premises of Mr C Boyce, of this town. Passers by and others were invited to witness the exhibition. On the afternoon of Friday they were drawn backwards in a waggon through the streets and thoroughfares of the town, proceeded by a banner, borne by two, with an inscription of 'God save the Queen' and followed by another with 'The Supremacy of the Queen for ever – Down with the Pope,' and incessantly saluted by the loud execrations of the numerous spectators. In the evening they were again brought out, and conspicuously placed upon the heath, and a waggon load of faggots and a quantity of tar piled round them, and then set fire to. Two pounds of gunpowder and other combustibles were confined in the heads of the Pope and the Cardinal, which upon being touched by the fire, exploded with a terrific noise, and were blown high into the air, amidst the deafening shouts of a large concourse of persons.

Catholic emancipation was obtained in 1829, when Catholics were admitted to Parliament and all property owning restrictions were removed. In 1850 the present English catholic hierarchy was established. Cardinal Nicholas Wiseman was created the first Archbishop of Westminster and the Pope established a regular diocesan system in England.

1851

4th January 1851

Ingratitude – Last week, while Mr Christopher Webb of Cheveley, was in Newmarket, he found a small basket, in which were a purse, containing 6s in silver, a pair of gloves, etc., He made no secret of it, on the contrary, he left word at a public house that if any person could give a satisfactory description of the property, he would gladly give it up. A Mrs Wicks was the person who lost it. She had it cried, and a reward offered. Upon hearing that Webb had found it, she wrote to him, and identified the property, which was immediately returned to her. Mr Webb was obliged to trouble a person to see to it, and promised him the offered reward as a remuneration, The man waited upon Mrs Wicks, who not only refused to give the proclaimed reward of 2s, but asserted that 2s or 3s had been extracted from the purse. Mr. Webb is exasperated at such unmerited calumny, and is desirous of proving to the public that the property was returned exactly as he found it, and that he never intended to have taken the reward for himself.

James Wicks, tailor, High Street. PO Directory 1847

1st February 1851

The members of the Newmarket Cricket Club (held at Mr Ralph Westley's the Golden Lion Inn) met on Monday evening last to audit the last year's accounts, and to appoint fresh officers for the ensuing season. The meeting was well attended, and from the spirited feeling evinced by the gentlemen present, the coming season promises to be one of great interest, and as the members have thought it advisable to increase the subscriptions of the honorary and playing members, it is to be hoped the Club will meet with that encouragement and support from the patrons of this manly game resident in the town, it has hitherto done. With an expanse of ground second to none in the Eastern Counties, and a Club composed of members who, by practice, may safely compete with their neighbours, surly we may anticipate pleasure both for the spectators and players. The officers appointed were – Mr Charles Frye chairman, Mr Ralph Westley treasurer, Mr Thos. Clarke, secretary, and a committee of five playing members. A vote of thanks was passed to the late chairman (Mr G F Peck) and the other officers for their services during the past season. We cannot give too much praise to Mr Thomas Clarke, the indefatigable secretary, for his anxious endeavours to forward the interests of the club.

1st February 1851

County Court – *Rogers and Clark v Chifney.* – This action was brought by the plaintiffs, who are stationers of this town, to recover the sum of £32 8s 6d of Mr Chifney, a training groom, for five years use and hire of a pianoforte. Mr Clark said that an agreement was made between him and the defendant for £6 a year, and the instrument had been changed several times during that period, at the request and for the accommodation of Chifney. Nothing had been paid whatever for the hire. The judge questioned Mr Clark as to his custom of letting out such instruments upon hire, and said that as neither the defendant nor any other person appeared to contradict Mr Clark's statements, he was bound to give him (Mr Clark) the judgement of the court. He (the Judge) knew nothing of the defendant's pecuniary circumstances but should give a verdict for £5 down and £5 a month. The plaintiff assured his Honour that the defendant was able to pay a greater sum down and as the debt had been standing a long time and nothing paid in liquidation thereof, he hoped his Honour would grant him £10 down and the £5 a month. Judgement accordingly.

Rogers & Clark, printers, booksellers and stationers, High Street. PO Directory 1847

15th February 1851

Pedestrianism – Frost, the well-known 'Suffolk Stag', displayed a series of his pedestrian feats at Newmarket, on Saturday last, as we have heard with out receiving much encouragement. Again, on Monday, he undertook to do the following within an hour: - He first ran a mile, in good style and comparative ease; then drove a wheel-barrow a mile, trundled a hoop a mile, walked a mile, in each of which he went a quarter of a mile out and in, from the Golden Lion to the lower end of the terrace in the front street; he then hopped 200 yards, jumped 60 yards in a sack, jumped the same distance with his legs bound together; picked up 50 stones at one yards asunder, which feat, according to arithmetical progression, is one mile and 790 yards; and finished by jumping over 60 hurdles, at six yards apart. Notwithstanding the many turns and necessary stoppages, he accomplished this extraordinary task in about 56 minutes.

1st March 1851

Attempted Burglary - On the night of Tuesday last, an attempt was made to break into the market shop of Mr Gent, situate in the Wellington Lane. It is supposed that the thieves were disturbed, as they only succeeded in cutting an aperture in the window shutter, through which a quantity of beef, mutton, and suet was stolen. This ought not to be attributed to apathy or negligence on the part of the police-constable, who, (without any sycophantic display) is considered a very indefatigable officer. One policeman is not a sufficient protection in so extensive a district. The evil disposed fellows of course watch his movements more than he can theirs.
William Gent, butcher, Mill Hill. PO Directory 1847. This is probably where he lived.

8th March 1851

A Company of about 40 of Prince Albert's Own 11th Hussars, arrived in this town, on Tuesday, from Ipswich, for the purpose of proceeding to Burwell to protect and assist the civil power in taking possession of the long-disputed Fen ground. They were not called out till Thursday, and then their services were not required, in consequence of a body of infantry, which arrived in Burwell previously, having succeeded in gaining possession, We should very much like to know at whose suggestion all this useless expense has

been incurred, and greatly fear that these displays will not inspire the poor with reverence for the law.
The fen edge village of Burwell, lies about four miles from Newmarket. Poor's Fen, used by the poor of Burwell for cutting turf (used as fuel) and sedge (used for thatching) for their households use, was ruled by Chancery to be let as a farm. The labourers receiving much sympathy locally objected to losing their traditional rights. Five hundred people occupied the disputed land, undeterred by police from Scotland Yard, to obstruct the construction preparing it for cultivation. They eventually gave way in the face of troops including Hussars.

17th April 1851

A new and effective mode of employing persons in clearing land of docks is adopted by most of the farmers in the neighbourhood of Newmarket. Instead of paying the men by the day or the acre, they now pay them at so much per stone, the pay ranging, according to the abundance or paucity of the weeds, mostly from 3d to 3½ per stone for the first time of going over the land, and 4½ d to 5d a stone for the second time of cleaning. This system has been found to work admirably, and is a source of satisfaction both to the farmer and labourer, as it encourages the latter to work hard and attentively and entirely frees the mind of the farmer from all diffidence whatever.

3rd May 1851

A Swindling Sportsman. – On Wednesday afternoon week, a scene of rather unpleasant and rare occurrence disturbed for a time the usual routine of business, and afforded no little merriment to the sporting characters on the race course. It appears that the town has been visited by a number of 'sharps' during the week and on Wednesday one of them, being gentlemanly attired, with a massive gold, or rather spurious, watch-guard suspended from his neck, succeeded in making a bet with Mr Boyce, a gentleman of this town, of £5 upon a race. Had he won, his purpose would have been effected. Fortunately Mr Boyce was the winner, and upon demanding the money found the sharper *incog.* had none, or other wise was determined not to part with it. He was at once recognised by a party as being the man who had attempted to transact business in the same manner at Epsom, where he was whipped off the course. He was almost immediately set upon by a number of persons who severely thrashed and chased him from the heath. In the evening, upon it's being known that he had taken refuge at the Greyhound Inn, a mob assembled, and demanded to have him given up. The police and other constables remonstrated with them, and endeavoured to disperse them, but in vain. The gates were repeatedly closed against them, and as often broken open. The landlord, finding it impossible to restore peace, was obliged to order the man to leave his house, when the poor fellow was escorted to the Golden Lion amidst the insults of the mob, who despite the interference of the police, literally tore his clothes from his back, and otherwise maltreated him. Upon entering the latter place his pursuers flocked in after him; but were eventually driven off by the landlord, through whose kindness he was during the night protected from other molestation. He left the town at the earliest opportunity.

Richard Boyce, trainer, Cheveley Road. Pigot 1839

14th June 1851

Whitsun Fair – This annual cattle fair, commonly called Whitsun Fair, was held in this town on Tuesday last, and was but modestly attended. The show of horses was far from numerous, but there was here and there one or two pretty animals to be found which realised very good prices. Neat stock was thin and not much in requisition. In the sheep department there was nothing like an abundance; the choicest and best were those exhibited by Messrs Gent and Wiseman, dealers, of Woodditton, which were of very good quality, and sold well. Taking the whole fair through, there was a thin attendance, both of dealers and cattle, compared with previous years, and trade was miserable dull, except with those who had good cattle to dispose of, which throughout made fair prices, but bad animals to use the dealers' phrase, could not even be given away, and many of them left unsold.

5th July 1851

The Order for the application of Public Health Act to this town, published on the 16th ult., by the General Board of Health, directs that the Act, except sec. 50, shall, after Parliamentary confirmation of the order, be applied to the town and such parts of Exning and Wood Ditton as are within the boundary line of Mr G T Clark's report; that the Local Board shall consist of 12 residents, possessed of property to the amount of £1000 and rated at £20 a year, one third to go

out of office yearly; the Hon. G Anson, MP, to be chairman for the first election; or, in his absence, Wm. Parr Isaacson, Esq., to perform the duties; to whom the notices of qualification of voters are to be given.

The 1848 Public Health Act, provided for a central Board of Health with powers to supervise street cleaning, refuse collection, water supply and sewerage disposal. The later acts passed responsibility to local Boards of Health and extended their powers to include drainage and sanitation. See 14th April 1855

12th July 1851

Annual Rural Sports. – These rustic sports were held upon the race course on Friday last. A great number of persons from the surrounding villages were in attendance, and the sports as usual comprised donkey, foot, and hurdle races, for sums varying from 7s 6d to £1. Races by boys, girls, and women, for boots, gown pieces, etc., jingling and rolling matches, jumping in sacks, climbing greasy poles, bobbing for oranges, and a series of other rustic games and amusements, which were maintained till a late hour in the evening.

12th July 1851

The Exhibition – On Monday last this town assumed a very dull aspect indeed, in consequence of all the tradesmen and persons of business having unanimously determined to close their shops, in order to afford to themselves and their assistants an opportunity of visiting the Great Exhibition. Several clerks and domestic servants of gentlemen in the town were allowed the same privilege, and upwards 200 passengers left Newmarket by the six o'clock train. We understand that one gentleman allowed his clerks £20 each for their visit.

The Great Exhibition opened on 1st May 1851 in a building of iron and glass erected in Hyde Park, London, commonly called The Crystal Palace. In the 24 weeks it was open it attracted upwards of 6,000,000 people. The entrance fee was 2s 6d on some days and 1s on others.

12th July 1851

Watering the Streets – The public have experienced considerable unpleasantness and inconvenience during this summer, upon market and other days, from an evil which we hope will ere long be suppressed. The tradesmen and inhabitants of the town are greatly annoyed, and many have had their goods damaged while being exposed for sale, owing to the dust which at this time of the year drifts through the town in dense clouds. Formally the streets were properly watered, but that remedy has been discontinued for some time past. On Friday last a public meeting was held for the purpose of considering what is best to be done to prevent the continuance of this great evil, when it turned out that the streets were formally watered, or, in other words, the expense of it defrayed by private subscription. It was agreed that the work be done by voluntary contributions, which would be further assisted by a gift of £20 pounds from the Turnpike-trust. A committee of five gentlemen was appointed to see it properly carried on. The meeting was well attended; S Y Benyon, Esq., of Stetchworth Hall, in the chair, and about £50 was collected in the room.

Before roads were macadamised the loose surface was a constant problem, muddy in winter and dusty in summer. Turn pike trusts were introduced in the 18th century to improve roads between towns, the trusts were allowed to charge tolls for the up keep of the new road. There was a toll cottage situated on the main roads at either side of Newmarket. The Turnpike Trusts that controlled the roads to and from Newmarket were:- Cambridge – Newmarket 1745-1874 (A45), Great Chesterford – Newmarket 1745-1871 (A11), Newmarket – Bury St Edmunds 1768-1871 (A45).

2nd August 1851

Special Train to the Great Exhibition – On Wednesday last the Newmarket Railway Company ran a special excursion train from Newmarket to London and back. The object of it was to afford those who have no friends in town, and perhaps not the means of defraying the necessary expense of staying in London the opportunity of visiting the World Fair, and returning in the evening, for the extraordinary low fare of 5s 6d per head. This privilege was further extended, each ticket was available up to and including the following Saturday. It was very evident that the Company were repaid for their kind attention to the public convenience, as it is currently reported that upwards of 500 persons were conveyed to London by this train. A fund was raised by voluntary contributions in Cheveley, Ashley and Woodditton, to which his Grace the Duke of Rutland gave £20, to enable the working classes to visit the Exhibition for 3s a head, the fund supplying the other 2s 6d and their admission into the Crystal Palace. From

about 180 to 200 availed themselves of these terms. The train left Newmarket Station at about a quarter past six in the morning and arrived in London about two minutes before nine, and left Shoreditch soon after eight in the evening and was in Newmarket before eleven.

Shoreditch was the London terminus of the Eastern Counties Railway, situated between Commercial Street and Bethnal Green Road. The station was erected in 1843 in an Italian style of architecture, approached by an incline from Bishopsgate. The Great Eastern Railway extended the line to Liverpool Street in November 1875.

2nd August 1851

Consecration – Considerable interest was manifested in Newmarket on Wednesday last, on the occasion of a visit paid to it by the Lord Bishop of Ely for the purpose of consecrating an additional piece of burial ground, the want of which had long been felt. His Lordship, accompanied by the Rev Dr Corrie and his chaplain, arrived at St Mary's Church precisely at eleven; and was received at the gate by the Rector and Churchwardens, who were supported by Clergymen from the neighbouring parishes, and a most respectable body of the laity. It was a pleasing sight to notice the arrangement of the children belonging to the Boys' and Girls' Schools. These occupied either side of the path from the gate to the porch, more than two hundred being present. Prayers having been devoutly said, with proper psalms and lessons for the occasion, the Bishop proceeded, with the clergy and as many of the numerous congregation as could face the heavy rain just then falling, to the burial ground, when the usual ceremony of solemn dedication and consecration were performed by His Lordship amid marked attention, Dr Corrie acting for the Chancellor. In this part of the service The Bishop was pleased to express his entire approval of all the arrangements of the day, which did credit to the parties concerned. After the conclusion of the ceremonies the Bishop and Clergy were invited to luncheon by Chas. Phillips, Esq., the senior Churchwarden, and His Lordship was on his return to Ely shortly after two o'clock.

This graveyard is situated in Church Lane that connects St Mary's Square with the High Street.

21st August 1851

Lusus Naturoe – Mrs Williams, a widow, of Newmarket, has a cat, which produced five fine kittens, on Monday last, all of which are joined together at the buttocks and living.

20th September 1851

Gun Accident – On Sunday morning last, a young man, Thomas Peck, carpenter, in the employ of Mr Westley, of this town, was out with a gun upon his master's lands, for the purpose of shooting small birds, upon discharging it in a horizontal position, it burst, and flew into a thousand pieces, many of which struck, and most severely wounded him in the head, laying bare one side of his face. His hand, arm, and other parts of his body were dreadfully mutilated, so that, should he recover, it is much feared that he will always be a cripple. A person happened to be near at the moment the gun was fired, and perceiving something had occurred, ran up to the unfortunate young man, and immediately had him conveyed home. He was examined by Mr Page, of this town, under whose skilful treatment he now is, who at once reported it to be a very dangerous case. The poor fellow soon became delirious, and his life is now despaired of.

27th September 1851

Accident – On Friday last, as Mr Heffer, dealer, of Exning, was driving from Moulton to this town, he was inadvertently looking another way at some sheep near the road, when his horse, which was proceeding at a rapid pace, suddenly fell down upon his knees cutting himself in a shocking manner, Mr Heffer, who is a heavy man, was at the same moment thrown from his cart with great violence upon the road, and sustained some serious injuries. He immediately drove to Mr Fyson's surgery, in this town, when it was discovered that his ribs and collar bone were broken. We are enabled to say he is going on very well.

22nd November 1851

Sudden Death – On Monday morning last, a widow woman, named Sarah Elsdon, of this town, went to see her daughter, who was living at Mr F Butler's and after entering the house, she complained of a slight pain in her chest, and immediately fell down dead. An inquest was held upon the body the same day, before Charles

Phillips, Esq., when a verdict of 'Died by the visitation of God' was returned. The deceased was 61 years of age, and had been under the attendance of Mr Gamble, surgeon, of Newmarket, for some time past for a disease of the heart.

29th November 1851

The Newmarket and Bury Railway. – The new line, for which application to Parliament is advertised, proceeds from Newmarket station, across the turnpike road about half a mile from the Bury entrance to the town, to Snailwell field, where it takes a curved direction to the south of the Water Hall, passes Kentford on the north, and again crosses the turnpike road near Higham, from which point it runs nearly parallel with the road through Barrow field and the two Saxhams to the north side of Westley Old Warren Wood, again crosses the road near the two-mile stone, and takes a direct course to the Bury Station. There is a short tunnel just after leaving Newmarket, under the Exercising ground, but, with this exception, the levels on the whole extent are extremely favourable, and the estimated expense is less than half that of the former line. Notice of abandonment of the former line has been given to the several landowners. The principle proprietors on the new line are Mr Tharp, Mr Godfrey, Mr Wellsman, Mr Barclay, Mr Mills, the Marquis of Bristol, and Mr Lee.
Powers for an extension of the railway from Newmarket to Bury St Edmunds were granted in 1852 and the line opened on 1st April 1854. The new line involved a tunnel under Warren Hill of 1100 yards in length. See May 1852

29th November 1851

Sheep Stealing – During the night of Friday last week, a sheep, the property of Miss Weatherby, was stolen from the fold, the skin, offal, etc., were left in the field. A reward of £10 is offered for the detection of the party, but up to the present time no clue has been obtained. A sheep has also been stolen from the fold of Mr Sabin of the Rutland Arms Hotel, in this town.

20th December 1851

Robbery & Confession – On Thursday night last week, the establishment of Mr Peck, surgeon, of this town, was thrown into an unusual state of excitement, in consequence of the windows of the house having been found opened, and the rooms occupied by the servants in a disordered state, chests of drawers were emptied and left open, boxes and other things strewed about in confusion, as if some one had been ransacking the room, and then made their exit with precipitation. Upon looking things over, it turned out that the housemaid had lost £5, and the cook 10s, and of course, every one was upon the *qui vive*, anxious, if possible, to detect the artful thief. It was thought probable that the 'unknown' might conceal himself in the adjoining house, which is uninhabited, for the purpose of availing himself of the stillness of the midnight hour; and of course, the keys and a policeman were sent for, and the house searched, but no traces of the thief were discovered. Upon more mature consideration, it did not appear at all feasible for any person to have entered the window, without first getting upon the roof, and then crawling over a bed that was standing close by, and as the bed had not been touched, and no other signs of ingress and egress were observable, it was at once suspected that the thief was still in the house, and a strict investigation was instituted, but the whole affair was, as yet, wrapped in mystery, till Mr Peck told the servants that if any one of them had taken the money, and would confess it, he would readily forgive them, and promised to continue them in his service. The cook then acknowledged that she had stolen the money, and had spent it, and that, to lull suspicion, had left the room in the state they had seen it; and as a blind, had pretended that 10s was stolen from her also. Cooky, who, by Mr Peck's promise, escapes from punishment, was very active in endeavouring to discover the thief, and actually held the candle while this place and that person was undergoing a search; and a short time since, when the medical assistant was apprehended, she wondered whatever could have induced him to commit the robbery, or succumb to such propensities, and if she had done so she could not live another hour.

1852

25th January 1852

Highway Robbery – Between five and six o'clock on Tuesday evening last, as Mr Charles Holmes and his wife, of the Links Farm, Stetchworth, were returning from market, and having got to the bye road leading to the farm, Mr Holmes got out of his gig to open the gate, which had been closed by some scoundrels, for the purpose of

compelling him to alight, and while in the act of unfastening it, three fellows at once fell upon him, and extracted the sum of £2 10s and his watch from his pockets, Mrs Holmes seeing the intention of the fellows, drove back to Newmarket and gave information to the police. Fortunately for Mr Holmes, no more property was found upon him, and great praise is due to his wife for her presence of mind in driving back to Newmarket, as she had above £100 in her pocket.

14th February 1852

Pedestrianism – On Monday afternoon last, a 100 yards foot race, for £10 a side, came off on the Bury turnpike, between Frost the 'Exning Star', and Petingall, the 'Newmarket Pet'. The road was cleanly swept, and stakes fixed down throughout the whole distance, for the purpose of supporting a rope to divided the course, to prevent the one running against the other. The morning was very unfavourable, but just about an hour before the time fixed, the solar beams broke forth resplendently, and hundreds might be seen wending their way from all parts towards the turnpike. Frost is quite a youth, and weighs about six stone; he was the first on the ground, and so great was the interest he excited, that numbers flocked round him, and much admitted his running symmetry. Betting now became brisk, at six to four on the 'Star', with few takers. Petingall looked pale and exhausted, from hard training, which strongly convinced the spectators which place he would occupy in the race. No time was lost in bringing them to the mark; a pistol shot was fired, and both bounded off at a rattling pace, when the 'Star' ran in an easy winner by about two yards. It was afterwards stated that Frost got the start, but it is quite evident that he is the fastest man. Time 10 seconds.

6th March 1852

An extraordinary day's sport with the Suffolk Fox Hounds took place on Thursday week. From the meet at Kirtlinge Tower, they proceeded to draw Ditton Park Wood, where, within five minutes, Sam's welcome cheer reminded each sportsman that a fox was on foot, who speedily broke cover, closely followed by his pursuers, through Fen Wood, skirted Widgeon's through Basefield, to the Ditch, where they lost him. Trotted on for Great Carlton Wood, and Lopham's, both blank; but at Hart Wood unkennelled a good fox; quick away for Carlton, the Widgeins, Ditton Park, and the Ditch, from whence (some contended with a fresh fox) back again to the Widgeons and Hart Wood again, where "'twas thought he must die," but the gallant old fellow still defied his pursuers, and retraced his steps by Carlton, the Widgeons, Ditton Park, and at the Ditch, was lost, being spared we trust, to run another day. Two Cambridgeshire sportsmen (unflinching supporters of the ex-Thurlow Club), the worthy master (J Josselyn Esq.,) his huntsman, and whip maintained their pre-eminence throughout this brilliant day's sport - *from a fortunate eye-witness.*

In or about 1790 the hunting county of Suffolk was divided and a fresh pack of hunting hounds called The Thurlow was started by Thomas Panton and kennelled at Newmarket.

27th March 1852

Conviction of Dugard – At Bury, on Wednesday, James Dugard (29) was indicted for killing James Betts, at Newmarket, in November, 1850. Mr Power was counsel for the prosecution; Mr Wm. Cooper appeared for the prisoner. At the Newmarket fair, in November 1850, Mr and Mrs Betts were accosted by a woman, and while they were endeavouring to get rid of her two men came up and picked up a quarrel with them; one of the strangers dealt Mr Betts a blow on the head with the butt end of a heavy riding whip, from the consequence of which the unfortunate man died in 10 minutes after he was found on the ground by a passer by named Port. For some time no trace of the ruffians could be found; but a man named Chappel Brand Newman, a well-known Cambridge thief, since convicted of burglary at Downham, in Norfolk, made a statement implicating himself and the prisoner in the transaction at Newmarket, which led to the arrest of the latter. As soon as Dugard was taken up he said, "All this comes of spewing of that --- -- Convict." When cross examined to-day, Newman gave a sad history of his past life, admitting that he had been in custody 12 times, and that he had made this charge out of revenge, because Dugard had deserted him in his extremity for the Downham burglary, and had not even "got him counsel, " though he had "bagged" about £100 by the sale of the proceeds of that affair. His Lordship, having left the whole case to the jury, they, after a brief deliberation, returned a verdict of "Guilty" and thereupon the

prisoner was sentenced to be transported for the term of his natural life.
John Dugard convicted at the Suffolk Assizes 23rd March 1852, transported on the Adelaide, that sailed on the 16th April 1855 with 260 male convicts to Western Australia. Arrived on the 18th July 1855. Deeks.

1st May 1852

County Court, April 23rd – Before J Collyer, Esq. There were 45 plaints entered, and 14 brought before the Court, but the following was the only one worthy of notice:- *Daley v. Sutton.* – The plaintiff, a training groom, of Newmarket, is the tenant of the defendant, a surgeon, of London. Claim, £7 15s, for work and repairs done upon the premises, as alleged, by order of the defendant. The learned Judge expressed his dissatisfaction of the evidence, and decided the case by allowing the Plaintiff £2 6s only, with leave for the plaintiff to move for a new trail upon the production of other witnesses.
John Daley, horse trainer, Jockey Lane. PO Directory 1847

8th May 1852

Deaths – At Newmarket 23rd ult. aged 63 Mrs Elizabeth Bonnett and on the 30th aged 56 Mr Samuel Foreman landlord of the Grosvenor Arms, and formerly boot and shoemaker Cheveley.
Samuel Foreman, Grosvenor Arms, Grosvenor Yard. PO Directory 1847

15th May 1852

Robbery – On the 5th instant, a tramp professing to be a journeyman carpenter, called upon Mr Josiah Marrow and solicited work, no doubt with the view of selecting something in the shop for his own profit, as the next morning six planes were missing. Superintendent Brown at once sent a description of the man to Cambridge and Bury. He was in consequence apprehended at Royston, with some of the planes in his possession, and taken before Magistrates at Arrington, and committed for trial.

15th May 1852

Wombwell's Menagerie – Newmarket was much enlivened on Tuesday last by the entrance of this celebrated menagerie. The band was very good, and we believe many visited the collection.

15th May 1852

Prize Fight - The usual tranquillity of this town was unexpectedly disturbed on Monday last by a disgusting and brutal scene called a prize fight, between two pugilistic heroes named Orme and Jones, for £100 a side. The party first met at Six Mile Bottom, and had a few rounds when there arose a cry of "the Peelers, the Peelers;" and about 200 heroes scampered away from four policemen; the fighting men having blankets thrown over their shoulders, and the railway carriages standing ready on the line close by to receive them. Many sanguine admires of a prize fight, who had raised early and travelled far that morning, were miserably disappointed. After being foiled in other attempts, and begging of one gentleman, and offering money to another, at Newmarket, to allow the fight to take place in their paddocks, to no purpose, they determined not to be done, proceeded to the neighbourhood of Mildenhall, but without success. They again returned to Newmarket, and had the temerity to form a ring on the Warren Hill, within less than a mile of the town, and succeeded in fighting 17 rounds before the police were appraised of their whereabouts. The officers were soon on the right scent, and eventually dispersed the belligerent mob, who returned to the railway station, took the four o'clock train to their first meeting place; but we are informed that the fight was not resumed.

Surely the most extraordinary involvement of the ECR was with the fight on 10th May 1852 between Orme and Jones for £200. A special train left Bishopsgate (renamed from Shoreditch on 27th July 1846) just after 8 am with a number of fight fans who believed they were only going as far as Chesterford. However they only stopped there to water the engine, proceeding forwards along the old Newmarket line (officially closed from October 1851!) to Six Mile Bottom. Orme was meant to be waiting there, but he had got wind of Police activity and so the special train (with ECR officials aboard) continued along the railway to Newmarket. At this point accounts of the event vary. It seems that Orme met the train at Newmarket, from where he piloted it back along the disused line to Bourne Bridge, having lost some of the spectators along the way. One source even suggests that Orme gave directions while sitting on the tender. At Bourne Bridge fighting started at last, but they had only reached Round 9 when the cry of 'Peelers!' went up. In the resulting furore, everyone could be seen 'making for the train and jumping into the first carriage he could find. The train reversed direction once more and everyone travelled to Warren Heath, just beyond Newmarket, where a further 23 rounds were possible before another Police intervention. So it was back to the train once more, Orme still giving directions from the tender. They travelled along the old line again, passing a detachment of Police who were waiting at Six Mile Bottom. They rejoined the main Cambridge to London line and continued to a point two miles south of Chesterford. Jones, rather than the Police, spoilt the proceedings this time. He said that he had thought the fight was abandoned and had therefore consumed some oranges and brandy while on the train. It may simply be that Jones had lost patience with this bizarre farce, as other reports say that he refused to get out of the train a third time. It was also said that the referee had resigned. But what did the Board of Trade think about such unscheduled use of a line which was at that time closed for general traffic'? - Paar and Grey.
[ECR – Eastern Counties Railway]

22nd May 1852

As Mr Kitchener, solicitor, of this town was out riding last week he fell from his horse, and is confined to his room in consequence of the injuries sustained.

29th May 1852

Railway Extension – The Preamble of the Bill for the constructing the line of railway from Newmarket to Bury has been declared proved by the Committee of the House of Lords.

19th June 1852

The first sod was turned on Monday last for the proposed Bury and Newmarket Railway. The event was celebrated by an elegant cold collation, with champagne in abundance. Cecil Fane esq., occupied the chair; and J Stuart, Esq., MP for Newark, was amongst the numerous company. The line is expected to be opened within fifteen months.

17th July 1852

The Rural Sports – These annual sports were held on the race course on Friday last, and consisted, as formerly, of donkey and foot races, rolling and jingling matches, hurdle races, etc., The children of the Union were allowed to be present, and a good supply of plum buns was distributed among them, and with which they appeared highly delighted. There was a vast number of persons assembled, and the Newmarket band enlivened the scene with their assistance.

17th July 1852

Lamentable Death ~ We are sorry to have to record that on Monday week, whilst Mr Calkin, the warehouseman at the White Hart, was unpacking some soda water, one of the bottles exploded, and severely wounded him about the temples and eyes that it proved fatal, and he expired on the Thursday following. Some pieces of the broken bottle were taken from his eye, from which the poor fellow suffered the most excruciating pain; and as we were informed at the time, after inflammation and mortification had done their work, he died. It appears from further inquiry, that the poor sufferer was perfectly sane and harmless, and that his ravings were effects of pain only; and although the strait~jacket was considered requisite, and kept on till he died, he continually begged them to remove it, stating that he did not require it; but his entreaties were in vain; and after struggling and writhing with pain for a long time during this excessively hot weather, he became exhausted and delirious, in which state he expired, leaving a wife and three young children unprovided for. The poor young widow was confined on Friday last, and is, we are sorry to say, in a very precarious state.

Yard of the White Hart

24th July 1852

Lost and Found ~ On Tuesday week last, as Mr John Holland, of Kennet Bell, was returning from Newmarket, when about a mile from the town, he missed his watch and returned to the Waggon and Horses to inquire for it but, not finding it there, had it cried, without success. Then again set off for his home, making up his mind to the loss, but having taken up Mr Cornell, a dealer, of Fordham and informed him of his loss, when they had got about half a mile out of the town Mr Cornell called out "There lies your watch!" and sure, enough, there it was in the middle of the road, where it had been lying full an hour, during which time a drove of cattle, and many persons returning from market, must have passed it.

7th August 1852

The Harvest ~ Several farmers in this neighbourhood have commenced wheat harvest;

many are mowing their wheat, and others using the reaping machine, thus entirely dispensing with the old fashioned tool. The sickle. In a few days the harvest may be said to be general. Every description of crop is in good condition, and promise well for an abundance. We are happy to say that up to the present, the potato crop in this district is quite free from the disease. A very heavy thunderstorm passed over this district on Wednesday last, and the rain poured down in torrents. The thunder and lighting were awful for some time; two horses at Newmarket were frightened by the tempest, broke from their driver, and galloped over a little girl at Newmarket, who is now in danger.

Although the mechanical reaper was invented in the U.S.A. in the 1830's, it was never used extensively here. Mechanical harvesting began to spread more quickly, after the American reapers manufactured by Hussey and McCormack were displayed at the Great Exhibition of 1851. From this report, it appears that farmers around Newmarket, were some of the first to try the new machines seen at the exhibition.

30th October 1852

The late fire at the residence of William Parr Isaacson, Esq., was a very narrow escape from the destruction of that fine mansion, and may serve as a warning against a modern practice which has frequently within our knowledge been attended with mischievous results. We allude to the practice of placing very low grates according to the modern fashion, so near the hearthstone that it actually becomes red hot, which was the case in this instance, and communicates the fire to the adjoining timbers.

In Georgian houses the fire grate was raised some distance from the floor, and consisted of a cast iron surround with a basket grate. Later Victorian fire grates were lower or at floor level with a tiled hearth in front.

4th December 1852

St Mary's Church – Through the efforts of several parishioners, this parish church has been reopened for Divine Service on Sabbath Afternoons and although the public only received notice of it last Sabbath Morning, in the afternoon there was a very good congregation. This will be a source of gratification to our diocesan who ordered that service be restored.

4th December 1852

Opening Dinner – Our readers will see by advertisement, that Mr Boyce's opening dinner, at the Rutland Arms, Newmarket, will take place on Tuesday, the 14th instant, and that there may be some festivities, in which the ladies may share, it has been determined to have a ball on the 21st instant. It will be seen by advertisement, that efficient stewards have been appointed.

The Rutland Arms stands on the site of an earlier inn called the Ram. The present building was designed by John Kent and built in 1815.

Accident – On Friday last, as a man named Dunn the ganger in the Bury and Newmarket tunnel, was clearing away some earth to allow the trucks passing, a portion of the side slipped in upon him and broke his leg. We hear that a short time since some of the horses, used in the tunnel, narrowly escaped injury from a similar cause. The tunnel is now rapidly progressing and has been partially worked through to the other shaft near the Bury turnpike.

The Post Office – A memorial to the Postmaster General is in course of signature, praying his Lordship to direct that some central premises in the town be provided for conducting the business of the Post-Office, instead of the present inconvenient situation near to the extremity of the town, on the road to the race-course and Cambridge. Amongst other facts stated in the memorial in favour of its removal to the centre of the town, it appears that since the Post-Office was removed to its present position, nine or ten years since, "the necessity for the change has been steadily growing by the rapid increase of the town in other parts, particularly towards the railway station, or the east end of the town, which is still in progress, while no extension has, or, from local circumstances, is likely to be made in that part of the town where the Post-Office is situated."

The area of Newmarket around the first station, stretching from Granby Street and Vicarage Road back to the railway line was called New Town. All Saints Road from Sun Lane to the railway was then called Station Road.

18th December 1852

Mr Boyce's Opening Dinner – The opening dinner of Mr Boyce, who has recently entered upon the Rutland Arms, Newmarket, was celebrated on Tuesday last, and was the handsomest affair we have witnessed for some time. Upwards of 70 gentlemen complimented the respected landlord by taking tickets, and he in return provided a very sumptuous repast, with splendid wines of every description during the whole evening, *ad libitum*, and a desert as handsome as could be produced. The chairman was S Benyon, Esq., of Stetchworth Park, who was supported by Messrs. Moody, Fairlie, Brown (Newmarket Railway), Ratcliffe, Gilson, Bottom, Hunnybun, Phillips, Kings, Bridgeman, Edlins, C E Brown, Chisholm, Marham, Stacey, and many other of the most respectable inhabitants of the town and neighbourhood, as well as the principal trainers and resident jockeys. The toasts were chiefly complimentary, and therefore it is unnecessary to report them at length... The Chairman left about ten, and Mr Ratcliffe was voted to the chair, under whose auspices conviviality was kept up for some time. Three professional singers from London (Messers Husk, Walker, and Holmes) charmed the company with their performances, and were highly applauded. The whole affair went off in capital style, highly satisfactory to the landlord, whose liberality, however, would, we fear, preclude the hope of profit.

25th December 1852

Sir R Faircloth has been elected a Fellow of the Royal College of Surgeons.

Inland Revenue – The officers of inland revenue attended at Newmarket on Monday last, to receive the arrears of taxes. Our readers will be sorry to learn that our highly respected surveyor, Mr R Talbot, is to be removed from this district. It is proposed to present him with a suitable testimonial, and those persons who would wish to further the object are respectfully requested to communicate with Mr Wilkinson, postmaster Cheveley, near Newmarket, to arrange preliminaries, etc.

Ball at the Rutland – This came off on Tuesday evening, and was a very splendid affair. Mr Boyce may congratulate himself on the number of his friends, who have rallied round him to wish him success in his new undertaking.

Petty Sessions, December 20 – Wm Tebbit, labourer Newmarket, was brought upon remand, charged with stealing lead from a stand on the Heath at Newmarket. Discharged.

1853

8th January 1853

Newmarket Petty Sessions Jan 4th before S Y Benyon, J Dobede, and J S Tharp, Esqrs., – Robert Reed, John Bilton, George Fuller and Thomas Newton, all inmates of Newmarket Union Workhouse, were brought up charged with refusing to work, and convicted – Reed was committed for 21 days, and the other three for 14 days, to Bury Gaol.

15th January 1853

We are pleased to observe that this town has not been behind hand in the efforts now being made for providing intellectual and moral food for the people. A Literary Institution has been set on foot by a Committee of Residents, and the result of their labours has been the opening of a reading room, and the laying the foundation of a Library which will soon come into play. Upwards of 60 names have already been inscribed on the subscription list, though this has only been open since the commencement of the year. The list of patrons includes the distinguished names of the Duke of Rutland, Lord Exeter, Lord Keane, Lord George Manners, Sir R Pigot, and General Anson. The interests of the large class of persons engaged in shops, offices, etc., has not been neglected, as the establishment of a second-class subscription for their especial benefit will testify. The Reading-Room was opened on the first instant; and hopes are entertained of turning the Theatre into rooms for the accommodation of the Society. The scheme embraces Reading-Room, Library, Lectures, and Museum, and we heartily wish it success.

Odd Fellows – On Thursday, the 6th instant, the members of the Loyal Beacon Lodge of Odd Fellows, M.U., celebrated their twelfth anniversary, when 40 sat down to an excellent dinner, provided by host Westley. The chair was filled by Jas Manning, the vice-chair by P G Prichard Cooper. After the cloth was removed the usual loyal toasts were given, after that followed 'The health of the Officers of the Order', next 'The Officers of the District.' Toasts and songs were given alternately, and a very pleasant evening was spent. The company separated at a late hour.

Jas. Manning, clerk to the Jockey Club, Kingston Square. Whites 1855

22nd January 1853

Annual Ball – The second annual ball of the Five Bells Assembly was held at that inn on Thursday last. The were about 40 present, and much pleasure was experienced by all, who freely enjoyed the evenings entertainment without that invidious feeling of distinction, each being determined that mirth and hilarity, unrestricted by formal etiquette, should reign predominant. The band performed admirably and the dance was kept up till daylight, when the mutual congratulations of the party were sufficient evidence that the wishes of all had been realised. We should be happy to see all similar meetings terminate with the like result.

5th February 1853

The Railway – On Friday last, a considerable portion of earth over the tunnel near the railway station, fell in and impeded the works on that side of the heath. Fortunately no further damage was done. A temporary fence was put round the dangerous part of the tunnel and an arch is now being carried on. Again on Monday, while the men were at dinner, several loads more fell in at the same place, completely blocking up the whole tunnel. This is a very fragile soil, and unless care be taken, some serious accident may be apprehended.

12th February 1853

Concert – A concert of sacred and other music was held at the Theatre in this town, on Thursday evening last, in aid of the National School Fund. The attendance was very large and attentive, and the music and singing very good, and we believe gave general satisfaction. – The same evening, a public ball was held at the Five Bells Inn, and was numerously attended.

Ball – It will be seen by advertisement that a public ball will take place at the Rutland Arms Hotel, on which occasion Jullien's band will attend. We suppose this is intended as some compensation for the disappointment experienced by the failure to get up a Freemasons ball, at Cambridge.

Exhibition of Poultry – Cambridgeshire, then, it appears, is to have an exhibition of poultry,

which will take place at Newmarket, on the 16th and 17th of June next. The prizes awarded will amount to £100. Prize lists and certificates of entry will be ready on and after the 25th March.

The Railway – The Newmarket Railway Company commenced running luggage vans from the Newmarket station to Bury St Edmunds and back on Monday last. A conveyance of this sort has been much needed for some time past, and many will, without doubt, avail themselves of this desirable public convenience.

26th February 1853

The Ball – A ball, was held at the Rutland Arms Inn, on Thursday night, the 17th instant, when 120 were present. Dancing was kept up till after bright Phoebus arose, Jullien's band was engaged.

Death from Exposure to the Cold – A poor man named Wake, of this town, died suddenly on the morning of Tuesday last. The deceased was unmarried, and much addicted to drinking, in consequence of which he was invariably divested of the necessary comforts of life. We are informed that he was sleeping in a loft at a public-house on Monday night, when his sufferings from the severity of the weather were so great that he awoke and went home where he was shortly after admitted, and soon expired.

Cambridgeshire Exhibition of Poultry – We are authorised to state that the Cambridgeshire Exhibition of Poultry, to be held in this town, will not take place upon the 16th and 17th June next, as specified in the advertisements, but is unavoidably postponed till the July meeting week. The poultry mania is very prevalent in this neighbourhood, and the admirers of the Cochin and other breeds are anxious to contribute their quantum, and if possible, to excel their neighbours, in producing the rarest and the best description of birds, and it is expected that at this show, the collection of birds, and attendance of visitors will be very great.

The Weather – For the last fortnight, the weather has been very severe, the thermometer, in many instances, having stood from eight to ten, and on Thursday night week, between 13 and 15 degrees below freezing point. The fall of snow is greater than has been known for some years, and on Wednesday night last, a fall, accompanied by a tremendous hurricane of wind, was experienced, and continued for some hours with unabated fury; and some gentlemen who were travelling between 10 and 12 o'clock, are of opinion that the violence of the combined elements was never greater, if equalled, within the memory of man; and it was with great difficulty, and unremitting exertions, that they surmounted impediments of the drifting snow. Around Cheveley and the adjoining parishes, the roads were impassable, and teams were compelled to return to their stables, and most out door work was suspended in consequence of the great depth of snow, which in many parts was upwards of six feet deep. Farmers were compelled to send out their men to clear the roads; Mr W Halls, Hall Farm, Cheveley, had 19 men cutting through the Cheveley and Moulton road, during Thursday; and the Rev J T Bennett sent a horse machine round for some miles for the same purpose.

5th March 1853

St Mary's Church – On account of the indisposition of the Rev J Robinson, no service was given in the morning and afternoon last week. We had to notice that All Saints was closed in the same manner on the previous Sunday, on account of the illness of the Rev J Taylor. Surely these reverend gentlemen in case of illness should endeavour to find a substitute, unless, indeed, the illness is sudden and unexpected.
Rev. Robert Robinson B.A., rector of St Mary's, Bury Road. White 1855. The newspaper got the initial wrong?

Suicide – This town was thrown into a state of considerable excitement on Tuesday last, in consequence of the report that Mr Bateman, the landlord of the Black Bear Inn, had committed suicide by shooting himself in his room, which turned out to be too true. It appears that Mr Bateman had shown symptoms of mental derangement for some weeks past, and it was deemed necessary to keep his razors, knives, and every thing by which he was likely to inflict any injury upon himself, out of his way. On the morning he committed the rash act, he appeared more rational, but was observed to be walking backwards and forwards about the house for some time, during which he contrived to load his gun, and about ten o'clock the inmates were startled at the report of the gun, and on going to the room, they were horrified at finding that the unfortunate man had destroyed himself. He had placed the muzzle of the gun against his cheek.

We understand that he had previously expressed a determination to shoot his two valuable horses and dog. Great must be the bereaved widow's distress of mind to witness her husband's sad end, at the very time she was suffering the most poignant grief for the loss of a valuable friend and brother.
Mr Bateman had not long been landlord, as the PO Directory of 1847 gives the landlord's name as Samuel James.

The Militia – Five young men from Cheveley have volunteered and were sworn in the militia on Thursday last. Others from Ashley and Dullingham were also sworn in at Newmarket.
The militia was used to supplement the regular army by providing recruits from its ranks. It was also used to keep civil order before the introduction of a regular police force. The militia was organised in county regiments, and the officers were gentlemen selected by the Lords Lieutenant of those counties. Because it was funded from the land tax, these gentlemen had a proprietary interest in the force.

19th March 1853

Instrumental Concerts – The Champness family gave their interesting entertainment, at the Assembly Rooms of the Golden Lion, on Wednesday evening, to a small, although respectable, audience. The performance elicited that applause which is but rarely given to persons professing to give an evening's amusement to the inhabitants of our town. The blending of the various instruments were equal to a powerful orchestra; and although the family consists of only four individuals, viz.; father, mother, son, and daughter, they were by the peculiar combination of their novel and splendid instruments, enabled to give forth sounds equal to a band of twenty performers. The evening concluded with a series of dioramic views, on a scale of great magnitude, and were through out much delight at the treat that had been afforded them; the only regret expressed was that the attendance was not what the combined talent of this family merited.
Golden Lion, High Street.

23rd April 1853

Daring attempt at Robbery – At about two o'clock, on Thursday morning, some ruffian attempted to rob the premises of Mr Hull, watchmaker and jeweller, of the above place. It appears that the robber effected his entrance by a window in the back yard, from thence he proceeded through the parlour into Mr Andrews' shop, which is only separated from Mr Hull's by a thin partition. Mr Hull slept in his shop, and was awakened at this time by his dog, and saw a man, with a dark lanthorn, attempting to pick the lock of his shop; he coughed, and disturbed the thief, who, made his escape the way he came, leaving behind him a screw-driver and rasp. We hope shortly to record his capture, and that he will receive the punishment he justly deserves.

21st May 1853

Whitsun Fair – This was acknowledged to be the finest and best fair in this town for several years. There was a large attendance of sellers and buyers, and also of pleasure seekers. A very fine display of good stock of every description: good cart and nag horses were much in demand, and met with ready purchasers, and many were sold. Neat stock numerous and fine, which, with milch cows and heifers, went off pretty well. Sheep plentiful, and a good sale, and many left the fair under new owners. During the fair, Mr Chapman's man, of Mildenhall, was a dupe to some sharpers, under the following circumstances: - It appears that this man was deputed by his master to sell a horse, which he succeeded in before his master arrived; and, while having some refreshment, a stranger, having the appearance of a gentlemen, accosted him, and congratulated him upon having sold the horse for more than his master anticipated, at the same time inquiring whether his master was yet arrived, pretending that they were intimate acquaintance, and had promised to meet him at the fair; the man answered in the negative, but expected him shortly; the stranger left, promising to call in five minutes – he did so, and appeared disappointed at not meeting his friend, Mr Chapman, but hoped he would soon be there, as he had made an unexpected purchase, and wanted his friend particularly; but if Mr Webb, of Eriswell, were there he would do, and requested the man to ascertain if he were come; upon learning he was not, he asked the man to lend him £16 of the horse money (being all, or very nearly all, he had, as we are informed) on account of his master, as he had not time to run down to the bank at that moment, and of course his master would approve of it, as he should make it right with his master directly he came to the fair. The poor fellow innocently gave him the £16 and upon Mr Chapman's arrival his

unknown friend and the £16 were *non est inventus.*

21st May 1853

Robbery – Early on Thursday morning the premises of Mr Taylor, draper, etc., Newmarket, were entered and two valuable Cochin China chickens stolen therefrom. Mr Taylor heard the fowls making a noise, and the thieves were disturbed, or in all probability the whole stock would have been carried off.
Cochin chicken, common name Chinese Shanghai, originally from China and primarily an ornamental bird, but well known for their mothering skills and sometimes used as foster mothers for other breeds.

28th May 1853

On Monday last, the above place was visited by Mr Hengler's Colossal Hippodrome the company performed to a very full audience both afternoon and evening. The performance was very good consisting of some excellent horsemanship, ascent on a rolling globe up an incline plane, and some clever performance on a slack rope. The evening's entertainment concluded with a slight sketch of the Kaffir War which was not done quite so well as we expected.

5th June 1853

Newmarket Bury Extension Bill – This Bill has passed the two Houses of Parliament, but we cannot learn whether it has yet received the Royal Assent. There is, however, of course, no impediment to its becoming law. A clause was added in the Lords Committee reducing the shares to £6. 5s, as agreed upon with the new subscribers. Every preparation is being made for the commencement of the works; so that we trust we may now really calculate on the speedy completion of the line from this town to the metropolis and the midlands and northern counties. The contract for the embankment on the Newmarket race-ground, advertised in our present publication is not connected with the Railway. – *Bury Post.*
The embankment on the race course was probably referring to the artificial bank instigated by Judge John Clark. This ran for five furlongs parallel to the Devil's Ditch, locally known as 'between the ditches'. Horses were run in the artificial valley and this was an attempt to foil touts from gaining information.

12th June 1853

Bury and Newmarket Railway – We rejoice to be able to answer that it is the intention of the Directors to turn the first sod for the commencement of the works on this line on Monday next at Barrow Bottom.

9th July 1853

Importance of Telegraph – The Times has a telegraphic dispatch from Newmarket merely to announce the departure of two horses for Worcester and the arrival of two others.

3rd September 1853

The Theatre ~ This building has lately been converted into a Public Hall and Literary Institution, and will be opened for the first time on Thursday next. It will comprise a very extensive hall and adjoining rooms, adapted in every way for public meetings, concerts, lectures, and other amusements for the million, and also a reading room, library, and committee room for literary purposes. We have no doubt that this change, from the trickeries of the stage to the truths of scientific pursuit and instructive amusement, will be much more agreeable to the inclinations of the metropolitans of the racing world and its numerous visitors than the offerings of the followers of Thespis have hitherto been. The Literary Institution is under the immediate patronage of the Duke of Rutland, Duke of Bedford, Marquis of Exeter, and other noblemen and gentlemen connected with the town; the members are already numerous, and there is every prospect of the continued prosperity on this pleasing undertaking.
See 11th Nov 1826

1st October 1853

The hurricane – During Sunday night the wind rose to a perfect hurricane, and was more violent than for several years past. Great havoc was done in the gardens; apples, pears, and plumbs, were completely stripped off the trees, and wall-fruit, exposed to the fury of the wind, have more or less suffered. Large oak, elm, and other trees and a number of young trees in plantations, have been blown down or broken off. Many sticks have been stripped of the thatch, and portions of the hay or corn scattered to a distance, and many lightly-built and dilapidated buildings have been blown down.

Newmarket and Eastern Union Railway – These lines may now be said to have been brought into contact, the chalk hill abutting on the station-yard of the latter having been cut through; and only about 20 yards of the embankment across the Tayfen meadow remaining to be completed. Much, however, is yet to be done to effect the junction of the two lines; but we trust that arrangements will be made for working the traffic in the present station, which will afford good and ample accommodation, sparing the public from annoyance and delay, and the Newmarket Company from useless expenditure in forming a separate station, as well as in the changes of management, which there can be no doubt that the efficient and experienced master of the Eastern Union station (Mr Dutton) would be fully competent to conduct, to the satisfaction of the town and the respective Companies, in the important developments of traffic from the Midland and Northern Counties (added to that from the Metropolis) which may be anticipated from the opening of this direct line of communication. The importance of this opening may be estimated when it is considered that Peterborough, where the Northern and Midland lines converge, will be reached, via Huntingdon, in little more than 60 miles, instead of the present circuit of 200 miles by London; and that passengers leaving this town at 8 or 8 30 a.m. will be able to reach Sheffield at 4, York or Leeds about 5, and Manchester at 8 the same evening.

5th November 1853

Turkeys – Her Majesty has acknowledged the present of the beautiful turkeys, from J Fairlie, Esq., by conveying her thanks to that gentleman, and expressing her desire to possess another hen bird to match them. It was accordingly sent to the royal aviary on the 27th ult.

Robbery – As a gentleman, who had been staying at Newmarket for the meetings, was walking home about 12 o'clock, on Saturday night, having been out to dine, when opposite the betting rooms he was suddenly seized, and his gold watch and money stolen from his pocket. The thieves escaped. We understand that he has given different versions of the affair, and did not appraise the police till the following Monday, just as he was leaving Newmarket.

19th November 1853

A frightful accident has occurred to Mr Thomas Randle, the active resident agent of the contractor for the extension of the Newmarket and Bury Railway. On Friday, whilst superintending the works at Kentford, he attempted to get upon the ballast engine when in motion, but the earth on which he stood giving way he fell upon the rails. With great presence of mind he rolled over on his side, or his life must have fallen sacrifice; as it was, the wheels passed so close to his body that his coat was torn into shreds, his back severely bruised, and the engine and several loaded waggons passed over his foot and ankle, literally crushing his bones. He was immediately conveyed to Newmarket, and it was found necessary to amputate the limb between the knee and ankle. The operation was most skilfully performed by Mr Faircloth, whilst the patient was under the influence of chloroform, the wonderful effects of which were proved by Mr Randle being unconscious that the operation had been performed until the fact was communicated to him after the effects of the chloroform had passed away. Mr Randle is progressing favourably.

The Newmarket surgeon Mr Faircloth, was using the very latest techniques of medical science on Mr Randle. Sir James Simpson, Professor of Midwifery originated the use of ether as an anaesthetic in childbirth in 1847. Experimenting on himself and his assistants in the search of a better anaesthetic, he discovered in November 1847 the required properties in chloroform. He championed its use against medical and religious opposition until used by Queen Victoria at the birth of Prince Leopold II, in 1853, signalling general acceptance.

26th November 1853

On Thursday, the 17th instant, a lecture was given at the Assembly Room, Newmarket, on the subject of 'Table Turning,' by Mr Edward King, formerly a medical officer, which was to be illustrated with a series of experiments. A correspondent gives us a miserable picture of the affair. The company was very limited, the room imperfectly lighted, and by some men and boys present, the table was eventually made to move round with surprising velocity. The table was told to perform various antics, such as bowing to the ladies and dancing, etc., but, every now and then, the 'wooden' pupil showed all manner of obstinacy, which, however, vanished, when a young gentleman with a brown wide-a-wake

and rough coat stepped forward and placed his hands upon the table; our correspondent insinuates that the affair was mere chicanery.

The County Court – Some extensive alterations and improvements have been made in the interior of this Court. Hitherto the body of the Court was enclosed by unpainted rails, and as there was nothing to point out the respective places for the plaintiff and defendant, much confusion and inconvenience were often experienced; and but little accommodation was afforded to the public. The last Court opened with a striking change in appearance and comfort. Around the centre table have been placed new forms, with backs and elbows, and equally comfortable seats have been placed in different parts of the Court for the accommodation of the more respectable portion of the public. Two boxes for the plaintiff and defendant are placed on each side of the entrance to the space occupied by the legal gentlemen, and directly opposite the Judge. The passage behind the jury seat, leading to the Judge's room is enclosed, which with other marked alterations, entirely preclude the public from encroaching upon that portion of the Court assigned to the officials. The porch and entrance to the Court have been modernised, and folding doors put up. The walls of the Court have been panelled, and tastefully grained and varnished.

Newmarket had two magistrate courts, because of its unique position on the boundary of two counties. The County Magistrates Court for Newmarket Cambridgeshire was held at the offices of Messrs Isaacson and Gilson in the High Street, on Tuesdays and Saturdays. The County Magistrates Court for Newmarket Suffolk was initially held on Saturday at Kingston House, All Saints Passage (now Kingston Passage). In 1856 a new court and police station was built in All Saints Road.

Novel Reform Society – We are informed that a novel society to be called the Parochial Reform Society is about being formed at Newmarket, each member of which is to have his own affairs closely and mutually scrutinised before intermeddling with those of his neighbour.

10th December 1853

Attempted Highway Robbery – As Mr George Bailey, carpenter, of Ashley, was returning home from Newmarket, at about six o'clock on Saturday evening last, when opposite the Railway Station, he was suddenly struck on the back part of his head, and knocked down. He immediately jumped up and struck the fellow a violent blow across the forehead and felled him to the ground, but had no sooner done so that he was pounced upon by two other men, who knocked him down again, knelt upon his body and throat, and ransacked his trousers, completely tearing them down, but in their haste overlooking his week's wages etc., which he had in his waistcoat pocket. Bailey was rendered insensible from the rough usage, and instead of proceeding home, unconsciously wandered across the exercising ground, and was walking all night, till he found himself in Moulton village, and did not reach Ashley till late in the morning. He thinks his first assailant must have been carried away by the other two, as the blow was a severe one.

Parochial Reform Society – It is the desire of many of the leading projectors of this society, that an influential inhabitant of the town will do them the honour of presiding at their opening dinner.

17th December 1853

Attempt at Highway Robbery – We have been informed that the account published under this heading last week, was circulated by Bailey himself, for the purpose of concealing his conduct which was disreputable. The police were not spoken to by him, although he alleged that he was stopped near the Railway Station; but they have since found out, that instead of wandering unconsciously to Moulton, he actually went there for the purpose of fighting a young man who well thrashed him for his trouble.

1854

14th January 1854

Snow Storm – The night of Tuesday week was one of the most violent and stormy nights remembered for many years past. The wind raged with unceasing violence till after noon on Wednesday. As soon as day break appeared the devastating scenes of the work of rude Boreas presented themselves. Trees and buildings overthrown by the impetuosity of the wind and driving snow. Every hollow completely filled with snow, and many roads filled upon a level, and in many places many feet above the hedges, and all traffic stopped; the letters by the mail cart did not reach their destination in the villages around Newmarket for many hours after the usual time, and the trains upon the railway were unable to run. Several dwellings were surrounded by the snow, and the doors entirely blocked up, so that the inmates had to dig themselves out, and the immense accumulation of snow in many places is between 10 and 15 feet deep; and so piecing was the wind and snow that in many cottages it laid some inches deep. Persons going to and from Newmarket were obliged to go miles out of their way, the road on the Cheveley side being impassable, and travellers on foot, horseback, and driving, had to pick their way across the lands. All farm labourers and surplus hands are engaged in cutting through the snow on the highways.

14th January 1854

Newmarket Association for the Prosecution of Felons – On Monday, the 9th inst., the members of the above society celebrated their anniversary at the White Hart hotel. The dinner was provided in Mr Bottom's first rate style; every delicacy of the season was upon the table, and the wines of the best vintage. The chair was ably filled by James Button Esq., solicitor to the association; the vice-chair by Mr J Daley. The chairman congratulated the society upon its flourishing condition having had but two cases of prosecution during the year. Loyal toasts and songs were given alternately and the evening was spent in a very pleasant manner. We must add that having so few prosecutions in the year, may be attributed to the vigilance of Superintendent Marson, of the Cambridgeshire police, and Sergeant Steggles of the West Suffolk police, both of whom are very active officers.
John Daley, trainer, High Street. John Marson, police inspector, Turf Terrace. James Button, solicitor, assistant clerk of county court, High Street. Thomas Steggles, police sergeant, Mill Hill. White 1855.

28th January 1854

Never too late – A few days since in Newmarket a couple on the 'shady side of seventy', who had lived together for thirty five years, and brought up a large family, were united in the bands of wedlock by the Rev J Robinson, the rector of St Mary's, Newmarket.

4th March 1854

NEWMARKET & BURY EXTENSION RAILWAY
IMPORTANT SALE

In consequence of the near completion of these Works,

Messrs ISAACSON & TATTERSALL

Have been instructed by Mr Thomas Jackson, the Contractor to SELL by AUCTION (without the least reserve), on TUESDAY NEXT, March 7th 1854 at the Railway Works, Newmarket;

TEN CART HORSES, Harness, Carts, Timber Carriages, large quantities of Earth Waggons, Trolleys, Blocks, Chain and Hemp Falls, a capital Mortar Mill, Crabs, Smith's Bellows, Anvils and Tools, Barrows, Wheeling Planks, Centres, Leggings, Temporary Rails, Scrap and Cast Iron, large quantity of White Brick, Stone, and Timber, and a general Assortment of Contractor's Plant. Also 50 pair of Hemp Sheets, 25 Coverlids, quantity of Bed Ticking, etc.,

The whole of which will be fully described in catalogues, to be had a week prior to the Sale, at the Railway Works; of the Auctioneers, at their Offices, Clare and Newmarket, Suffolk; and of Messrs TATTERSALL, Hyde Park Corner, London.

Order. – The Sale to commence punctually at Eleven o'clock with the Timber, Waggons, Horses, Harness, etc., Bricks, Stone, and General Stock.

29th April 1854

County Court – At the County Court on Saturday. Stevens v. Towell this action was to recover £2, for damage done to the plaintiff's gig. The plaintiff, formerly a veterinary surgeon, of Newmarket, said that in January last, he was driving the defendant out in his gig, and gave him permission to smoke his pipe the fire from which blew round and set fire to the lining and back of his gig. The defendant, at the time, promised to make it right, and advised him to send it to Mr Parker's coach repository at Cambridge, to be repaired. He did so and Mr Parker's bill was £3, £1 of which was for extra repairs ordered by him, the plaintiff. The charge for repairing the damaged parts was £2. The defendant denied this, and said that the charge for the damaged parts was only £1. Plaintiff agreed to take £1.10s. Order accordingly, with costs, in three weeks.

Henry R Stevens, veterinary surgeon, Cheveley Road. Pigot, 1839

29th April 1854

The Fast Day – Last Wednesday was most strictly and religiously observed in this town and neighbourhood. Every kind of business was entirely suspended, and the churches, both morning and evening, were crowded. Excellent and appropriate sermons were preached in All Saints' and St Mary's, followed by very liberal contributions towards the fund for the relief of the wives and families of the solders. Divine Service was performed, in the morning and afternoon, in every parish church in this district, and at many of them collections were made. It was supposed that in compliance of the Queen's proclamation, there would be a general cessation of business and labour, and we are informed that such was the case in this town and the neighbouring agricultural villages, with the exception of the parish of Woodditton, where as we are credibly informed, two or three of the leading farmers had their men and horses at their usual work upon their lands and farms, whilst even the little agriculturist and tradesmen displayed their innate feeling of loyalty and patriotism, and with the rest of their neighbours, observed the day as becometh true Englishmen.

The Crimean War 1854-1856. Britain and France declared war on Russia in March 1854. Britain and France feared Russian expansion into Europe. The 25th April was appointed by the Government to be a day of humiliation and prayer on account of the war.

6th May 1854

Board of Health – The operations of this board have been so active that, on walking round the town the other day, we perceive at the end of Sun Lane, a sack doubled over a grating which is placed over the common sewer. This means of preventing the escape of miasmatic effluvia is somewhat novel. We did not in our rambles, perceive any other stench traps of this invention; we suppose, therefore, the one we have eluded to was merely placed there as an experiment, and we have not yet heard the report of the trial. – Correspondent.

12th August 1854

Blind Reading – A novel exhibition was afforded the public in this town, on Tuesday last, by the reading of a man totally blind. The volumes from which he read were raised characters, not letters, consisting of an admixture of Harding's short hand notes and phonography, which he read feeling with accuracy and rapidity. Upon any person selecting a chapter or verse of any portion of the scripture from a common Testament, he would instantly turn to it in his own books, and reading it off with the same ease and time, by passing his fingers along the lines, as a good reader would from sight.

The system of reading using raised-point writing was invented by Louis Braille [1809-1852] in 1829.

9th September 1854

Runaway train – As some of the men employed on the Newmarket and Cambridge Railway, were removing the coal trucks, near the Dullingham Station, Wednesday last, three of them, containing 24 tons of coal, started to move off down the line, being a declivity, to Newmarket, the weight imparting an impetus sufficient to increase the speed to about 20 miles an hour, by the time it reached Newmarket, where it was stopped at the end of the line, fortunately, with no further injury than the smashing one of the trucks.

16th September 1854

The Assessed Taxes – The Commissioners of Assessed Taxes for the district held their annual meeting at the Rutland Arms Hotel, on Friday and Saturday last, for hearing appeals from persons assessed for service employed in attending their horses or carts, etc., Some who were employed were willing to pay for their horses claimed exemption for their carts, as they were used for business only, but upon being questioned, admitted they had driven to Newmarket to make their complaint, which the Commissioners intimated had rendered them liable. Others, who could not prove that they always cleaned their own horse, gig, or cart, were compelled to submit. Mr Turner, harness–maker, of this town, appealed upon the ground that he attended his own horse and cart himself, except upon one or two occasions, when he had taken his cart to one of the inns to be washed by the ostler, and for which he was informed he must pay the full charge for a servant.

Joseph Turner, saddler, High Street. PO Directory 1864

7th October 1854

The Cholera – During the raging of this dreadful visitation in the metropolis and other parts of the kingdom, this town and district were, till last week, entirely free, with the exception of its concomitant diarrhoea, which may be said to have been rather prevalent. The Sanitary Board and authorities in the adjoining parishes, have neglected no part of their duty in enforcing cleanliness yet, notwithstanding their unremitting endeavours to ward off this dangerous epidemic, it has at last found its way into this generally healthy little town. Last week a young man, said to be on a visit from London, died after a short attack of cholera. A bad case broke out in one of those miserable pent up alleys near the 'Rookery.' On Sunday, the patient, a brewer, named Parr, took no notice of it in its earliest stage, and on Monday it became more virulent, with cramp, and on Thursday morning he expired, leaving a widow and large family. On the same day, a woman, named Elsden, died of the same dire disease. We have not yet heard of any more cases.

Cholera: a highly infectious and often fatal intestinal disease. The first outbreak occurred in 1831-33, introduced into the country through the north-east ports from Russia. Further outbreaks occurred in 1848-49, 1854 and 1866. On each occasion the disease spread with alarming rapidity, largely because of the lack of proper sanitation. The outbreaks provided a spur to public health legislation.

21st October 1854

The Cholera – We are sorry to say that this dreadful disease has at last made its appearance in this town. There have been three or four fatal cases during the last eight or nine days. A young man, named John Linwood, a bricklayer, was attacked on Sunday morning last and died in the afternoon, and was buried on the following day. Another man was found in some straw in a paddock. His groaning attracted notice, and it was found that he was unable to speak, but was at first though to be drunk. The fatal cases of Cholera have occurred in those pent up dwellings around the 'Rookery' the majority of which are thickly inhabited and subject to filth and stench. Inefficient drainage is considered to be the predisposing cause.

25th November 1854

The Fair Removal – Some of the inhabitants of this town complained to the magistrates of the long standing of the various stalls and shows after the recognised three days the fair supposed to exist, and obtained an order, which was printed and circulated, amongst the people holding the fair, and posted upon walls in many parts of the town. It had the desired effect with many, who as soon as possible left this town fearing to incur the punishment consequence upon the disobedience of the official mandate. Other intrepid dealers in fancy goods, treated the order with contempt, and had the temerity to throw down the gauntlet, and challenge the authors of the bills to a test of right or wrong in their attempt to abolish a time immemorial custom of standing up to or over the market-day succeeding the third day of the fair. Summonses were accordingly issued, and served upon twelve of the party who thus persisted in maintaining the right of custom, and on Tuesday last the Court of Petty Sessions was crowded by persons to hear the majority of whom were inhabitants of the town, anxious to hear the whole case from beginning to end, an ample report of which appears in our Petty Sessions page of this day. The decision proves that the Bench had no authority to issue the orders of removal; and show more clearly the feeling of the town in this respect, it ought to be remarked that persons whose property is more or less encroached upon by this fair, actually strove to maintain the right of custom as here disputed; and after the action was settled, although in favour of the customists, a subscription was immediately set on foot for the purpose of defraying the legal expenses of this charge, and readily met by many in the town. Although these notices were circulated for a clearance on Saturday, the actual termination of the fair did not take place till four days after. The magistrates, giving their opinion, intimated that the desired object was obtained in the removal of the fair to another part of the town in future, but even in this there seems to be some doubt as to the legality, as the contemplated alteration will remove the fair from its original spot into another parish and county. But by the decision of the Bench on Tuesday, should the fair be removed to the so-called fairstead, we hear the stall-keepers intend to hold their ground.
The Fairstead was by St Mary's Square.

23rd December 1854

Christmas Market – Every department of this market today (Tuesday) was a cheering animation, it was in reality a resuscitation of the good old bygone times, and the preparations for this festive season in every necessary ingredient for the larder and cellar were numerous. The butchers had done their part in catering for the public, their shambles groaned under the weight of abundant supply of excellent meat of every sort. The display of beef and mutton, was truly wonderful, and that exhibited by Messrs. Bocock, Gent, and Holmes, attracted much notice, and of the very best quality. In particularising these, we do not in any way mean to depreciate the display or quality of the others, but on the contrary, must frankly confess, that they received their quota of public admiration and support, merited by the excellence of their stock, and considering the particular manner in which the meat was exhibited, the selection of joints, to their fancy, by the public, and the active and obsequious conduct of the butchers, imparted to this portion of the market a really pleasing and picturesque appearance. In taking leave of this scene of plenty, our paramount wish was, that before the butchers close their shops to participate in the festivities of the season, they might have the pleasing duty of serving the poor as well as the rich; and as Christmas comes but once a year, we most sincerely trust, that no poor family will have the mortification of seeing it pass without a joint of meat upon the table. The fishmonger, poulterer, fruiterer, grocer, and confectioner, all vied with each other in displaying a redundancy of good articles, their exertions, we hope were amply rewarded. Even the innkeepers were not behind and adding to the many requirements of Christmas, and that attention might be duly called to their extra-superior supplies, bills announcing such facts, were put into the hands of the public on their way to market.
David Bocock, butcher, Market Street. PO Directory 1864. Nine butchers are listed in White's 1855 Newmarket Directory

1855

3rd February 1855

The War – Several young men from this district have volunteered from the Cambridge militia into different regiments of the line. Into whatever one enters nothing is spoken or thought of but the absorbing subject of the war, and the most ludicrous epithets are being applied to the Emperor of Russia, and awful indeed would be his fate were all parties able to wreak the vengeance of their feelings upon him. We heard an old fashioned gentleman suggest a course of treatment; " I think said he, the severest and *profitablest* punishment England could *flict* on the old *Caisar* (Czar) when they get him, would be to confine him in an iron cage, and carry him about to all the fairs, and make a show of him all over England, as they do the wild *baste*, and lots of money would be *cumulated* that way, and help us with the war expenses, as the poorest man would willingly pay his sixpence just to have a squint at him. *Arter* they have done with him here, they could play the same game with him in France."

In the Crimean War much of the allied efforts were directed at the Russian fortress of Sebastopol. In September 1855 the Russians withdrew and hostilities were formally concluded by the Treaty of Paris in March 1856.

Panton House next to the present Post Office, was divided into three residences; the part that formed the house on the corner of the High Street and the Avenue, was called Cardigan Lodge, the residence of Lady Cardigan, whose husband played a major role in the Charge of the Light Brigade.

3rd February 1855

Inquest – An inquest was held at the Grosvenor Arms Inn, Newmarket, on Monday last, before G A Partridge, Gent, Coroner, on the body of Frances Holgate, 73 years of age, who was found dead in her bed. There being certain rumours prevalent in the town as to the circumstances of her death, and the house in which she died, situate in Grosvenor Place, not being a very reputable one, and it being a fact that money supposed to be in her possession was not forthcoming, it was deemed expedient to have a post mortem examination, which set the matter to rest, and showed by the evidence of Mr Gamble, that death was the result of apoplexy, the deceased suffering from diseases both of the heart and brain, and the jury returned a verdict that deceased died of 'Natural Causes'.

10th February 1855

The Weather – During the heavy fall of snow last week several low roads became impassable from the immense accumulation of drifted snow, piled up for miles together in the most fantastical wreaths, in many places four and five feet deep, and above the hedges. For upwards of 200 yards beyond the Station, from the town, pedestrians were compelled to walk knee deep in the snow, or go a considerable distance out of the way, the officials of the parish having been rather tardy in clearing the road; and even now that some attempt has been made, there is just room for a waggon to go and for two to pass it is out of the question. It was a matter of some contrivance on Tuesday for vehicles meeting between the Railway Station and the White Bridge to avoid accident in getting to and from the town. One was obliged to drive down a declivity off the road and wait for the others to pass, or wedge themselves in a niche where the snow was not quite so deep, and when an opportunity offered make the most of it to extricate themselves form such a labyrinth. Surely in such cases the high roads ought to be cleared much wider for public convenience. We have been induced to expose this from the loud and numerous complaints of those who have experienced much difficulty in travelling and not from insidious motives.

3rd March 1855

Roper's, the Scavenger's Search for a Wife – This worthy, a diminutive queer looking, and most eccentric character, named James Parrot, but better known as 'Old Roper,' has been employed as scavenger in this town for some years past, and may be seen daily driving his donkey and cart through the streets in quest of manure, and every particle of refuse that can be obtained; and as this conspicuous vocation brings him so frequently before the public we may safely aver that he is well known to all the visitors of Newmarket, and therefore presume that a concise account of his connubial enterprise may be in some degree interesting. Having just buried his second wife, and considering a man without a woman like a ship without a helm, he determined to try his luck once more at least, and after making some fruitless overtures to several of the fair dames in his own locality proceeded to the Board of Guardians for assistance. Being admitted, and his business asked he stated that having lost his wife, and feeling lonely with out one, he was come to ask the gentlemen to allow him to go over their House, to pick out a wife. This, of course excited some laughter at the Board, to some of whom the eccentricity of Roper was known, and told that there was Old Betty So-and-so he might have if he could persuade her. "Oh!" said Roper, "She won't do; I want a more respectable woman than she. I don't want people to choose a wife for me; if you'll allow me I'll pick for myself, and take her home upon trial, and if she suits me, I'll use her well, and take pretty good care she don't come back here to be any more trouble to you; but if I don't like her, I shall bring her back, and take another, and so on, till I can get one that will do." Roper thought a month's trial would be requisite, which created some merriment; but was good humouredly informed that such a course could not be permitted, and consequently no one was subjected to this probation. Roper, not to be done, still persevered, and having taken a wider range for his gratification, soon fell in with a blooming young damsel, named Ann Halls, about 24 years of age of Kennet. Roper is about 54, but the disparity in their ages was amply made up by the bride elect being the mother of a baby between two and three months old. They were duly asked in Church, and on Monday last, just three months that day since the late wife died, were married at St Mary's in this town. This amour afforded much scope for the gossip of the neighbourhood, and some time before the hour appointed for the wedding, a crowd was collected near the house. The party did not go to church in the usual manner but Roper and the "Daddy" were there first to sally out, and after the lapse of about ten minutes, were followed by the bride and bridesmaid, each party being closely followed by scores of persons, bent on playing jokes. During the ceremony, some hundreds congregated in the vicinity of the Church, and so great was the excitement, that if possible to break the pressure of the mob, poor Roper was compelled to take one route, and his wife another from the Church; and it required all the efforts of the police to preserve order. The whole street was lined with hundreds of persons and nearly every window had its occupant; and this unique party was lustily cheered, and at times saluted with snowballs from the more reckless. Notwithstanding all this, we hear that Roper had a merry wedding, plenty of eating and drinking – as one party gave him a piece of beef, another some mutton, grog, etc., and the oddest wedding party ever seen in this town broke up about seven o'clock the next morning.

31st March 1855

THE LAY OF THE LUCKLESS ONE.
NEWMARKET.
Come listen now ye Topers all,
That love the flowing Can;

And warning take by my downfall,
For I'm a downcast man.

Oh! I have spent my time and cash,
With Publicans and Sinners;
But they have settled now my hash,
And dish'd me of my dinners.

At *Horse and Groom* I owe a bill,
The *Horse Shoes* an arrear;
I've help'd to fill their tills until
I've not a *Shoe* to wear.
Horse and Groom, Bury Road, George Flatman
Horse Shoes, Albert Street, Benj. Chas. Planner

To pay my tribute to the *Crown*,
I've parted with my toggs;
And going oft' to the *Greyhound'*
Has brought me to the Dogs.
Crown, High Street (Suffolk), Frederick Lynch Bloss
Greyhound, High Street (Suffolk), Wm. Jarvis (posting)

The *Black horse* being thoroughbred,
Of course I could not shun;
And I have had my face quite red
From sitting in the *Sun*.
Black Horse, High Street (Cambs), Betsey Barrett
Rising Sun, Sun Lane, Matthew Witham

The *Fountain* clear – for me had charms,
But now I taste the dregs;
And when at night I left the *Arms*,
I could not keep my legs.
Fountain, Fountain Alley (Rookery)
Rutland Arms, High Street (Cambs), Wm Dixon Boyce

I liked the beer at the *Black Bear*,
The brewing of Old Bruin;
The *Star and Moon* both Sireus were
To lure me on to ruin.
Black Bear, High Street corner of Black Bear Lane, Julius Pierre Bohn
Star, High Street corner of Sun Lane, Elizabeth Snell
The Half Moon, opposite the Terrace, Francis Day

There was a time I used to think
The *White Hart* was a deer (dear);
But there I cannot get a drink,
My heavy heart to cheer.
White Hart, High Street (Suffolk), Charles Bottom

The *Old White Lion* grins at me,
And mocks me as I pass;
The *Golden* one is gilt I see,
With portions of my brass.
White Lion, Albion Street (Rookery)
Golden Lion, High Street (Suffolk), Ralph
Westley

The *Marquis* fain would frown me down,
Now I'm of tin bereft;
I've been so loyal to the *Crown*,
That not a half one's left.
Marquis of Granby, Granby Street, Leonard
Ruse
Crown, High Street (Suffolk), Frederick Lynch
Bloss

The *Waggon* keeps its easy pace
With slow and steady team;
The *Railway Tavern* is the place
For getting up the steam.
Waggon and Horses, High Street (Suffolk), John
Martin
Railway Tavern, now Carpenters Arms, All
Saints Road, John Lovick

The Drivers there can drink and sleep,
They care not what I feel;
Full well they know I cannot keep
My cart upon the wheel.

They fleec'd me like a silly sheep,
To swell the *Woolpack's* treasure;
And if I in the *Bushel* peep,
They *Strike* me with the *Measure*.
The Woolpack, Drapery Row (Rookery), Robert
Parkinson
The Bushel, Drapery Row (Rookery), John
Mainprice

Not one of all these *Jolly* ones
Will stand a pint of *Stout;*
I tried it on at the *Three Tuns,*
At last they tu(r)ned me out.
The Three Tuns, Market Place (Rookery), James
Clark

Speed well the Plough's a good old toast,
With me a favourite sign;
The *Elder Bush* I lov'd almost
As well as Elder Wine.

I lov'd the *Duke of Wellington,*
As all good Britons do;
But now my Wellingtons are gone,
Aye! and my Bluchers too.

Duke of Wellington, Wellington Street, before
1815 was Fox and Goose, Fox and Goose Lane,
Robert Jacob

The *Wheat Sheaf* yields me nought but *chaff,*
There once my lap was full;
Too late I find I am a Calf
For going to the *Bull*.
Wheat Sheaf, Icewell Hill, Samuel Pearson
Black Bull, High Street (Suffolk), Ann Smith

The *Lamb* is too genteel for me,
A choice expensive dish;
To see the *Dolphin* makes me feel
As dry as any fish.
Lamb Inn, Market Lane (Rookery), John Palmer
The Dolphin, Market Lane (Rookery), James
Tomlin

I once was notic'd by the *Swells,*
But now they shrink from Me;
I think as now I pass the *Bells,*
One soon will pass for me.
The Five Bells, St Mary's Square, Robert Moody
Hassall

To all my former friends I've been,
But cash or grog I drew none;
My last appeal was to the *Queen,*
My next will be the Union.
Queen Victoria, Mill Hill, James Fras. Deeks

Fordham   J R WITHERS
Poem written by James Reynolds Withers, who
lived at Fordham, just east of Newmarket. The
landlords/ladies are from White's Directory 1855

14th April 1855

Board of Health – At length, after a lapse of
three years and a half, this Board have
commenced their works, and adopted a scheme
designed for providing a complete sewerage of
the town and improving its sanitary condition,
the streets being broken, and old brick sewers
emptied, etc., preparatory to laying down
earthenware tubular pipes throughout the town,
and at an expense of upward £2500, without a
supply of water. Whether this will be effectual
there are considerable doubts with persons well
informed on the subject; however, it is well that a
beginning is made.

Curious Accident – Some excitement was
created upon the race-course on Tuesday last, in
consequence of a singular accident, which very
nearly cost a person of respectability, named
Derisley, his life. As the horses in the Newmarket

Handicap were approaching the chair, they, from a continual 'crossing and jostling' uncommon here, contrived to force the 'Crown Pigeon' up so close upon the cords, that he and the jockey were precipitated over amongst the spectators. Neither the horse nor the rider was injured, but Mr Derisley sustained considerable injury, and many others were much frightened.

19th May 1855

The spring meetings, the dullest ever remembered, were brought to a close on Thursday last. The company both in the town and upon the race-course was remarkably thin. The dullness of these meetings is generally attributed to the elite of the sporting world being engaged in the Crimean War. As Mr Greville's Pyrrhic was passing through the town on Wednesday, it fell into the deep cutting made for the main sewer of the town, about two feet wide, and between ten and twelve feet deep, which has been left open more than half the length of the principal street, to the great danger and inconvenience of the public. The poor animal fell with two of its legs and body wedged in the drain, and the other two above it, and so great was its agony that its shrieks were dreadful. After considerable difficulty it was extricated by means of ropes, but so much injured that its recovery is doubtful. It is reported that Mr Greville insists on being indemnified for his loss.

Accidents - Mr Greville's 'Pyrrhic' which fell into the deep cutting for the main sewer of the town, last week, has since died. This drain is about two feet wide and between ten and twelve feet deep, and has been left open more than half the length of the principle street, to the great danger and inconvenience of the public. Since the accident some little has been done, by the erection of a few poles and rails in the front street, to prevent a similar one; but it appears that the works have been carried on in a very reckless manner, and the complaints from every quarter, against an evident indifference to the public safety, are both loud and numerous. Very deep cuttings have been made in New Town and, on Thursday, a child named Quince fell in, and was so seriously injured that the doctor has little hopes of its living.

9th June 1855

Accident – As a horse breaker was driving a young animal through the street on Tuesday, a dog barked and ran between the horse's legs and so terrified it that it instantly plunged across the street and dashed in at the gate leading to the betting rooms, and by a sudden and violent jerk extricated itself from the break, and ran up the yard with one of the shafts hanging to the harness. Neither the horse nor the man received any injury.

23rd June 1855

Inquest- On Wednesday last an inquest was held at the Horse Shoes Inn, before Charles Phillips, Esq., coroner, on view of the body of Thomas Shurmur, groom for Messrs Greville and Payne, the person who was riding the horse Pyrrhic, which fell into the deep cutting made for the main sewer of the town, during the spring meeting. It is supposed that his death was occasioned by some injury received from the fall. Only one witness was examined, but his statement did not tend in any way to prove the likely cause of death. A *post-mortem* examination was made by Messrs Faircloth and Peck, but their evidence was not heard, as it was deemed necessary to adjourn the inquiry for a week, to Friday, the 29th inst., in consequence of Mr Page, the deceased's medical attendant, being out of the country. Mr Kitchener, of this town, appeared to watch the proceedings on behalf of Mr S Clark, the contractor of the drainage of the town.

8th September 1855

Suicide ~ The most painful excitement was occasioned in this town on Friday morning last, in consequence of a report that Mr Thomas Pask had committed self destruction by hanging himself, and which, we are sorry to say, proved to be true. The deceased carried on an extensive, and to all appearances, a flourishing business, as a draper, and silk mercer, and was a loving and an affectionate husband and father, a well-disposed man, of sober and methodical habits, and highly respected by all who knew him. He was at all times appeared serious and reserved in his manners, and for some weeks past was noticed to be in a more nervous and desponding mood, especially since the death of one of his children, and between seven and eight o'clock on Thursday evening he was observed to be walking backwards and forwards repeatedly by himself upon the pavement in the street near his shop, having actually persuaded his wife to leave home for the purpose of seeing her sister, living in opportunity; and no doubt judging from the circumstances of the case, he committed the rash act almost immediately after she had left the house, as he was not seen by any one after that time. Having returned from her sister's Mrs Pask became greatly alarmed at his absence, and every inquiry was made in the town, but no one had seen him, during the night the house and premises, excepting the shop, were searched, but to no purpose. After a night of sad apprehension and anguish of mind, poor Mrs Pask's worst fears were realised, and the morning's light disclosed the melancholy fact that she was a widow. It then struck one of the servants that his master had taken the key of the shop on the previous evening, and on forcing one of the windows, he was discovered hanging from one of the balustrades. Assistance was soon procured, and the body being cut down, the medical gentleman were of the opinion that life had been extinct for several hours. The last acts of the deceased were sufficient to prove that he was a determined hypochondria for, having locked himself in the shop, to avoid suspicion of interruption, he took the key from the lock, pulled off his hat and scarf which were carefully laid on one side, and unbuttoned his collar, and swung himself from one of the chairs. An inquest was held the same evening before Charles Phillips Esq., when after hearing the evidence of the servant and shopmen, Mr Page explained to the jury that the deceased's brain was in a morbid condition, and had been for some time more or less affected, and they accordingly returned a verdict of 'Temporary Insanity'. Nothing has transpired to account for this lamentable affair. His loss is lamented by every respectable family in the town, and the warmest sympathy is felt for his young widow and children.

Thomas Pask, draper, High Street. White 1855

27th October 1855

Fairs – His Grace the Duke of Rutland, lord of the manor of Newmarket, has issued a notice that the Newmarket fairs will henceforth be holden on 'The fair stead' only, and that no booths, stalls, or stands of any description, will be permitted on the streets, highways, through fares, or wastes of the town.

15th December 1855

Exhibition – Monsieur Desara is exhibiting his celebrated Parisian troupe of histrionic dogs and

the same street, evidently watching an monkeys at the Public Hall in this town, on Thursday, Friday, and Saturday last. The performance gave satisfaction and was witnessed by all the gentry and clergy of the neighbourhood.

1856

16th February 1856

The position of the Newmarket Post Office has long been a grievance, from its great distance from the centre of the town. The Post Office authorities, on a representation of the fact, had promised to remedy the evil whenever the office should become vacant. The Postmaster had lately resigned; a successor has been appointed and the new Postmaster has purchased the premises of the old Postmaster. The inhabitants, therefore, have memorialised the Postmaster General on the subject.

Newmarket Post Office is first mentioned in our newspaper reports in October 1807. George Rowning is listed as Post Master in the Newmarket Directory of 1823/4 and also in Pigots of 1830. The Post Office in 1830 opened at eight in the morning and closed at nine thirty at night, but would continue to receive letters until ten by paying a penny or until eleven by paying sixpence. By 1839 the Post Master was William Le Pla, who held the post until the 1850's. He had the same office hours but opened at seven in the morning during the summer months. In the 1841 census William Le Pla, listed as Post Master, lived next to the Star Inn in the High Street. Although the Post Office, as suggested by the December 1852 report, appears to have been situated on the edge of the Cambridge side of the town, most possibly beyond The Terrace and much to the inconvenience of the customers. This state of affairs lasted until the mid 1850s. A report in the Bury & Norwich Post of the 13th February 1856 suggests that the new postmaster should consider 'two commodious houses one formerly the Post Office in the very centre of town'. See August 1856

16th February 1856

A Daughter's Sympathy – At Bow street Police Court on Wednesday last, Cornelius W J Harvey, a clerk at the General Post office, was fully committed for trial, charged with stealing many letters. One, amongst others, was found at his lodgings, which he purloined above a week ago, but which he had not opened, containing a remittance of 6d from a poor seamstress in London, to her still poorer mother in Newmarket.

23rd February 1856

Militiaman Enlisted – On the 5th instant, a young man named Samuel Hursk, a private in the Cambridgeshire Militia, on furlough at Cheveley, presented himself in plain cloths to the recruiting corporal of the Grenadier Guards, stationed at Newmarket, for enrolment into that regiment. He was asked by the corporal whether he did or had belonged to the Militia, and answered in the negative, and after the usual questions or challenge in enlisting took the shilling. He then but too late, acknowledged that he belonged to the Militia, but refused to give his name, and defied the corporal to do anything in the matter. The Commander of the Militia, at Ely, refused to grant Hursk's discharge, and consequently instructions were issued from the Horse Guards for his apprehension. He was taken into custody, and brought before a magistrate on Saturday, and remanded till Tuesday that the case may be decided by the full Bench. He is liable to twenty-one days imprisonment for the trick played upon the corporal in civilian's dress, and a further six months for wilfully defrauding the Government.
The majority of recruits were enticed by the entrancing rattle of the drum and the power of the spoken word, lavishly supported with drink. Colonels of regiments were given 'beating orders' which authorised them 'by beat of drum or otherwise to raise so many men as are to be found wanting'. A potential recruit would be given 'the Kings shilling' as a mark of his commitment, and would then be medically inspected before being attested by a magistrate. Richard Holmes.

Mysterious Loss of a Money Letter – Considerable excitement has been occasioned in this neighbourhood, in consequence of Wm Collin, the walking postman, employed between Cheveley and Kennet, through Moulton, Gazley and Kentford, having been charged with stealing a letter containing a sixpence. It appears that some complaints had been made respecting the loss or delay of a letter a short time ago, but through whose dishonesty or carelessness it was lost we are unable to surmise; but by judging from what was already known of the particulars of the case, and of the antecedents of Collin, the suspected party, we may, and ought in justice to him state most emphatically that in the opinion of the most respectable portion of this district, and the public generally, he is anything but the guilty party. The letter for which he was apprehended was a fictitious one, posted by Mr Neale, the Post Office surveyor, at Moulton, the last Office at which Collin received letters. It was remarked to him that there were two money letters, and he then returned them, and requested that a memorandum should be made of them, not that he suspected a conspiracy against him, but in consequence of unpleasant rumours, and to make sure that the letters passed safely from him. Does this in any way look like the conduct of a guilty person? He walked from within a few yards of the office where he received these letters, to within a few yards of the office in which he deposited them, with two respectable men, who were witnesses in his favour. At the Cheveley office, another man, not on the best of terms with Collin, takes charge of the unlocked bags at seven o'clock, and, according to his own evidence, did not deliver them at Newmarket till eight o'clock. The question might and would have been asked of this witness, if Collin had been represented by a solicitor, where he was during the interim of receiving and delivering the bags, as it is very evident that he could drive from Cheveley to the Newmarket office in less than half-an-hour. After the loss of this letter another fictitious letter, containing money, was posted by Mr Neale, and directed to be left at the Bell Inn, Kennet, for a Mr Power, a dealer, till called for. Collin had charge of this, and as it passed no other hands, it was honestly left and Mr Neale found it right. Collin was suspected of stealing the letter of the previous evening, his person and cottage were searched by the police, but nothing transpired to confirm the suspicions; and the readiness with which he answered the interrogation of the officers, and the voluntary manner in which he afforded every facility to them in the inquiry, and his unhesitating admission to Mr Neale that there were money letters received by him at Moulton, convinced every one of his innocence. The Surveyor was quite right in instituting an inquiry, but the manner in which the plot was managed proved a failure. The examination of the letter bags should have taken place at the Cheveley office immediately after they were left by Collin, instead of at Newmarket office; and then if Collin had left the letter at Cheveley, the bag might have been searched again at Newmarket, and then if the letter was about, the party would at once have been detected. The warmest sympathy is felt for Collin by the majority of the public, and a petition in his favour has been drawn up, and signed by the principle residents in his rounds and transmitted to Her Majesty's Postmaster General, praying his Grace to reinstate him in his situation, and we sincerely hope he will not lose it, as he has a wife and five young children to maintain.

This report highlights the distance that Victorian postmen had to walk to deliver letters. In 1858 a letter carrier was paid 14s to 18s per week which was considerably more than a farm labourer got, this was not a job to be put into jeopardy.

Newmarket with twenty receiving houses had the largest Penny Post in East Anglia. Trout records nineteen of these (or perhaps twenty as he notes Swaffhams in his list and this could refer to both Prior and Bulbeck which may have been served by one or two receiving houses) were set up in 1834 and 1835. Of these offices, eleven or twelve were in Cambridgeshire the other eight in Suffolk, nearly all of these would seem to have been served by probably three foot postmen on rounds to the south and east of Newmarket, the fourth round being just to the north of the Cambridge Road including Bottisham, Burwell and the Swaffhams and Exning. E A Postal History.

1st March 1856

Death of the Rev R. Robinson. – A gloom has been cast over this town in consequence of the death of the worthy rector of St Mary's. The deceased gentleman expired on Monday evening last at his residence, 'Heath House' Newmarket, after a short illness of inflammation of the lungs, leaving six orphans to lament his loss, having lost his wife a short time ago. The Rev rector officiated twice at his parish church on Sunday week, when he appeared to be labouring from a severe cold, to which he was much subject, and from which he had been suffering for several weeks. The poor have lost a great benefactor and the church a stanch supporter – *Correspondent.*

8th March 1856

Loose, the messenger from Newmarket to Wickhambrook, wishes to state to the public, and those that have thought proper to interfere with the matter, that he is authorised by the Inspector of the Post-Office to sort his letters on the road, as he has to distribute them himself in the district of Dalham, there being no Post Office there, and from thence to Wickhambrook; but as regards the Cheveley bag he has nothing to do with, only that he takes it from the Cheveley office a little

after seven o'clock, and leaves it at the Newmarket Post office, at eight o'clock, being the time allowed him. The friends of the Newmarket postman think it only right to state to the public that, during sixteen years he has been in Her Majesty's service, no complaint has been made of his conduct till his connection with the Cheveley Post office.

The late Rev R. Robinson – The remains of this lamented gentleman were interred on Friday last, and as a mark of the unfeigned respect entertained for him, the shops were closed, and a general cessation of business observed. The funeral sermon, a most impressive discourse, fraught with salutary advice from the departed pastor to his flock, was preached in St Mary's church on Sunday evening last, by the Rev Mr Sweeting, the curate. As soon as the church doors were opened, every available space was quickly occupied, and many to evince their respect for the deceased gentleman were from a want of room, content to stand even within the precincts of the church, so long as they could obtain a word of the sermon. The rev preacher was deeply affected, and many of the congregation were in tears. The most distressing circumstance connected with this bereavement is the fact that the six small orphan children are left entirely without any pecuniary resources, in fact penniless; but we are happy to say that the most influential and affluent of the town and neighbourhood are engaged in raising a fund by voluntary contribution for their support. On Tuesday last, the clergy and gentry of the district, met to consider what step should be taken, and before separating they generously contributed upwards £200 towards the contemplated fund. We believe that a list is lying at the bank for the names of those who may feel disposed to contribute their donation of charity, however small it may be. Two sermons on behalf of the orphans will be preached in St Mary's, and we believe All Saint's also, in this town on Sunday next.

3rd May 1856

Pedestrianism – Match against Time – On Thursday last, William Spooner, a well known pedestrian, appeared on the Newmarket and Fordham road, leading from the back premises of the Crown, to walk 20 miles within three hours. Some hundreds of the sporting world and gentlemen of high standing were on the ground. Martin Starling, the race course keeper, was deputed to ride in front of Spooner, for the purpose of clearing the road and seeing the distance was honestly walked; but long before the distance was gone over Starling's horse gave way and a second one was necessary and procured, which, with his rider, at the end of the 20th mile had had enough of it. Now and then parties would go a mile with Spooner, but to do so they were forced to run by his side or behind him. The odds, 5 and 6 and even more were laid out in favour of the walker. The match commenced at 20 minutes past 10, and the first mile was clearly walked in about 8 minutes. At the end of the first hour he had gone over seven miles, and appeared as fresh as at starting; and the remainder of the distance was walked at the rate of about a mile in 9 minutes. The 20 miles was completed in 2 hours and 57 minutes, Spooner appears a first rate walker, and was attended by Ned Smith and the Regent Street Pet from London. Several hundreds of pounds were staked on the event.

31st May 1856

Palmers Trial – The result of Palmer's trial was known in this town, by electric message, by five o'clock in the afternoon of Tuesday and was the source of general satisfaction.

Dr William Palmer, born in Rugeley 1824, was publicly executed in Stafford in front of 30,000 people at 8 am on June 14th 1856, for murder of John Parsons Cook in Rugeley at the Talbot Arms. Palmer became known as the Rugeley Poisoner. This message must have come on the railway telegraph as the road telegraph line did not arrive until 1859.

19th July 1856

Complimentary Dinner – On Friday evening last the clerks and staff of this station sat down to an excellent supper, provided for them at the Rutland Arms Hotel, by the worthy landlord, Mr W D Boyce. To commemorate the return of Mr Codling to the post of Station Master, he having been removed for a shot period to Trowse. The chair was occupied by Mr Challands, and a very pleasant evening was spent, all present contributing to harmony and conviviality, and the good feeling that was shown of the present Station Master. The company retired at 'early dawn' highly delighted with the treat afforded them by the liberality of the friends and supporters of Mr Codling, who, during the short period he had been at Newmarket, previous to his removal had gained for himself great respect

by his obliging conduct in the discharge of his duties of his office.

Francis Challands, malster, corn and coal merchant, agent to the Globe Fire and Life Insurance Company, High Street. PO Directory 1864

19th July 1856

Inquest – An inquest was held in this town on Monday, the 14th inst., before G A Partridge, Esq., Coroner, on the body of John Smith, aged 62, gardener at the White Hart Hotel, who, on the Saturday afternoon, went to the bar and asked for some ginger and water, and died almost immediately afterwards. Mr Pennington, assistant to Mr Peck, surgeon, was called in, and was of the opinion that he died of disease of the heart, which he knew he had. Verdict, 'Natural Death.'

19th July 1856

Accident – On the 1st inst., as Mr James Bartholomew, jockey, Newmarket, was riding on horseback he had a severe fall, receiving some serious injuries. He was insured in the Accidental Death Insurance Company, from which Society he will, during illness, receive £5 per week.

James Bartholomew, jockey, Mill Hill. White 1855

26th July 1856

Accident – On Thursday week, as James Mould, head porter at the railway station, was assisting in removing a hogshead of sugar upon the platform, one of the floor stones suddenly broke, and his leg was drawn in between the edge of the brickwork supporting the pavement and the cask in such a manner that the whole weight, about 16 cwt, was thrown upon it, literally crushing the bones and the flesh below the knee. The end of the platform where the accident occurred is flagstones, six feet square, supported by about an inch bearing from the edges of each stone upon brickwork, thus forming as many chasms between 16 and 18 feet deep, into which the poor fellow and the cask must have fallen together had it not been for the presence of mind of another porter, named William Butcher, who immediately fastened a rope round his body, and directed others to hold it secure while he procured levers, and by manly exertions succeeded in raising the pressure of the cask, which instantly fell through the opening with a tremendous crash. While these operations for extracting the leg were going on, the groans and shrieks of Mould were dreadful; and after the rope was so fastened as to prevent his falling, the greatest care was required to move the cask in such a manner that it did not carry away a portion of the leg in its fall. Fears were at first entertained that the bones of the leg could not be adjusted, and that amputation would be resorted to, but we are glad to say that, through the skilful treatment of Mr Faircloth, of Newmarket, the leg will be spared, and the poor man is progressing as favourably as can be expected. Mould has been very unfortunate having but a few weeks previous resumed his work, after some months' illness; but we are happy to say that his family will be provided for, as he has been so far provident by joining two clubs for the relief during affliction.

2nd August 1856

Post Office – The Post Office has been at length removed into the Wellington Lane thus affording very material convenience to the whole town. The Postmaster would have engaged a more conspicuously situated house in the front street, had there been one at liberty, and we believe he will do so at the first opportunity.

The Market – For the last two or three weeks, our market has been either dull or cheaper in the wheat trade, but no alteration in the price of flour except an advance. On Tuesday last, the value of wheat was rated from 4s to 6s cheaper, still the millers held out and refused to lower the price of flour. Last Friday the London market was written lower, and on Saturday some parties surprised the neighbourhood by announcing a rise of a penny a stone in flour. This was so glaring that many, even sellers, refused to accede to it. The price of flour is now 2s 10d and 3s per stone, and the labourers wages from 10s to 11s per week. This price of flour is a source of much dissatisfaction to the public and in many large poor families have suffered great privations. We cannot conceive a reason for such a policy as the millers have now adopted. Wheat is considerably cheaper in proportion to flour; in fact the latter is at present selling as dear, if not dearer than when the former was between 10s and 12s higher, and this too, in the face of as an abundant harvest of every kind of crop, ever remembered.

16th August 1856

The Comet and the Meteors – There has been much gossip in this neighbourhood relative to the appearance of a comet, and various meteoric coruscations, lately witnesses have given rather a mysterious corroboration to the rumour, and set thousands of persons star gazing. We have been informed, on good authority that one poor woman, on going to the shop, did not think it necessary to carry home her accustomed weekly quantity of goods, as she had been given to understand that a dreadful storm and tempest were to take place, and the world was likely to be destroyed very soon, in consequence of the great comet; and on hearing that a young man named Charles Pavis, of Cheveley, had been alarmed on his way home, on Saturday night, by the appearance of a singular figure, resembling a funeral procession, with a corpse borne by four men, which preceded him about four yards off, for some distance, a certain person was heard to say that "It was another instance of many proofs that the scriptures were being fast fulfilled – that there must be wars and rumours of wars, and that young men are to see visions."

23rd August 1856

An Impostor – On Saturday last, a tall, strong fellow, dressed in the garb of a sailor, with a few tracts in his hand as an excuse for begging, was making a round in this neighbourhood, and by a plausible and well studied tale of misfortune and distress, representing himself as a shipwrecked sailor, having belonged to a ship wrecked about six weeks ago, and illustrating his account by exposing a sickening sore upon his right leg, which he described as a wound received by the bursting of the boiler and engine in the ship. Having received his reward for relating his deceitful narrative, he immediately opened a second petition for shoes and cloths on behalf of an equally unfortunate mate, who he pretended, was gone forward on the road in an almost naked condition. At a gentleman's house in the neighbourhood he was fortunate enough to obtain a good sum of money, and a bundle of good clothes, which were soon sold, and the proceeds spent in drunkenness. On applying for relief at Cheveley, and exposing his wound, he was at once recognised as an impostor.

30th August 1856

Post Office – This town has been placed in a state of considerable excitement for some days, owing to the intended removal of the Post Office a second time. The office was removed about two months ago to a central situation, which appeared to give general satisfaction; although situated in a Lane, still it was considered by all the inhabitants to be quite central; but it appears there are persons in the town who are determined that it shall not be so, from the fact that the Postmaster has actually taken a house at the same end of the town as the old office was situated, where the population is small, besides being a remote distance from the centre and business part of the town. Active measures are being taken by the inhabitants either to prevent a removal, or compel the postmaster to remove it to a more central situation than the one intended at present, there being at the present time three houses to let in the front street, all eligible for a Post Office. The Postmaster General has been written to and an Inspector sent down to survey the town, so that it may be placed in a central situation, in accordance with the general wishes of the inhabitants. A petition has been sent to the Postmaster General, signed by the principle people of the town.

In the 1851 census the property next to the Star Inn was not listed as the residence of the Postmaster. Presumably Mr Le Pla had moved to another address as he was still listed as postmaster in the Whites directory of 1855. The next reference is in the 1861 census for Cambridgeshire, All Saints. The property next to the Star Inn becomes the Post Office and the residence of the Postmaster who was Julius Bolin aged 37 and his wife Emma aged 30. The PO Directory of 1864 lists Henry Andrews as Post Master at the Post Office in the High Street. Peter May maintains that the Feathers Public House became the 19th century Post Office and was bombed in 1941. (See September, 1860)

29th November 1856

A Telegraphic Agent – In the Court of Bankruptcy last week, before Mr Commissioner Phillips, Thomas Hogg came up and described himself as a 'telegraphic agent', and said his occupation was to send messages by the telegraph to gentlemen of the arrival of horses at Newmarket. He was not connected with any betting office. Mr Sargood, who opposed for a Newmarket creditor, said there was no pretence for the description of 'telegraphic agent'. Mr Phillips held that the description was bad. It might mean any one connected with the telegraph office. Seeing where the creditors resided, he advised him on the next occasion to try Newmarket. The petition was dismissed.

6th December 1856

Marriage – The nuptials of Henry Hughes, Esq., of Worcester, with Matilda, second daughter of William Parr Isaacson, Esq., of this town, was celebrated at All Saint's church, on Thursday last. Long before the time appointed for the ceremony, the most respectable inhabitants of the town were wending their way to the Church, anxious to secure a sitting, and equally desirous of testifying their unfeigned respect towards the amiable and accomplished young lady, so well known to all and whose urbanity and kindness of disposition had endeared her to every class. Proper arrangements were made at the Church, through the directions of J Button, Esq., churchwarden, to secure accommodation, and although the public were not indiscriminately admitted, the Church was quickly filled. The ceremony was performed by the Rev Jas. Isaacson, rector of St Mary's, and uncle to the bride. The happy bride was conducted to the altar by her father, attended by sixteen bridesmaids, whose rich and superb dresses were the admiration of all. The bride was dressed in a splendid attire of white satin, with deep lace hangings and flounces, tastefully embroidered with bridal devices and trimmings of rich texture. Her head dress comprised a beautiful and almost natural wreath of orange blossoms, adorned with spangles over which was thrown a large white lace veil. Her retinue of ladies, with valuable adornment to correspond, and their heads encircled with an imitation of holly, in unison with the season, and heath brake, and fen wreaths, and white veils, corresponding with that of the bride. The marriage procession consisted of eight or ten carriages, and both servants and horses were dressed in bridal knots. During the service, the best order was observed both by those fortunate enough to gain admission and the patient crowd in the church yard, who notwithstanding the severity of the weather kept their standing round the entrance of the church, while others crowded the windows, and as soon as the happy couple emerged from the sacred edifice as man and wife the assembled crowd cheered them most vociferously. After the marriage had been solemnised, the party proceeded to the residence of Mr Isaacson, where a splendid and most sumptuous breakfast was provided, and partaken of by upwards fifty of the elite of the county. After breakfast, the bride and bridegroom left Newmarket for Nice. The same night a grand dinner and ball were given at the mansion of Mr Isaacson, and was most numerously attended.

13th December 1856

Mr J Barret, late of the Black Horse Inn, was interred in All Saints churchyard on Wednesday last. His remains were followed to the grave by many inhabitants of the town, and several of his companions and friends anxious to pay their last tribute of respect and the funeral procession was headed by a number of Odd Fellows, of which order the deceased was a member.

Betsey Barrett, Black Horse. White 1855

20th December 1856

Judge Clark and the Turf – We find that Judge Clark, of Newmarket, has acted in his official capacity in four hundred and ninety six cases. In these races, that he has judged, not less than 3,323 horses have started. – Era.

JOHN CLARK
Judge of the Course at Newmarket, 1834

Judge John Clark was judge of racing from 1852, he was by profession an architect who designed a number of local houses. He lived in Warren House. His father was landlord of the Greyhound Inn and had also been judge of racing.

Francis John Clark, architect & surveyor, Fairstead House. White 1851

1857

21st February 1857

Accident – As the ostler at the White Lion was driving a gig belonging to Mr Parker, of Weston Colville, down the street, on Tuesday afternoon last, it took fright and ran off at full speed, and the wheel of the gig came in contact with a bricklayer's hand cart and broke the axletree in two, and the ostler was thrown out and received some injury to his head. The pony still dashed on, in spite of many attempts to stop him, till he came against a gig, that was fortunately stopped at the time, which in some degree checked him, when, to avoid the crowd that appeared in front of him, he suddenly made for a stall of oranges and sweets, and jumped upon it, completely smashing bottles and other articles containing goods, and as he was going on, with the gig, across the stall that was levelled to the earth, he doubtless would soon have upset the large stall of Mr Reynolds had he not been seized at the moment. A little girl sitting upon the stall narrowly escaped, and the gig was uninjured.

John Reynolds, fruiterer and greengrocer, Market Place. PO Directory 1864

7th March 1857

Newmarket – *Bad Money* – Several pieces of spurious coin have been passed in this town and vicinity during the last month and as a considerable number have been circulated, the public, and every person in business ought to be particularly cautious in paying and receiving money. These counterfeits may with little attention, be detected in several ways. They are prepared in such a manner, in many instances, that a casual receiver, without using a proper test might not observe them. In both gold and silver imitations, they are devoid of the legitimate ring, and may be detected in weight, and where the colour approximates the genuine one, they may be perceived by a greasy and slippery handling, or rubbing against one's teeth, but in the majority of cases, the colour is sufficient to detect them, especially when placed in juxtaposition with good money.

Warren Hill – At this season of the year the visitor and inhabitant of this great racing town enjoy no greater treat than a morning's walk over and around the spacious exercising ground. On one side of the hill may be seen groups of the first-rate horses of the day leisurely perambulating the flat; others, perhaps, are gently trotting and prancing, with all the pride and spirit of high mettle; while on the opposite side a line of horses may be seen, taking a long gallop over the hill. In the centre distance, are numerous groups of equestrians, on first-conditioned animals, surrounded by pedestrians presenting a very picturesque scene, and representing a really colossean riding school.

21st March 1857

Burial Board - Meetings have been held by the ratepayers of this town, for the purpose of adopting plans, and making the necessary arrangements for the future interment of the inhabitants of the town. A board, composed of nine from each of the two parishes has been formed, and agreed that the parishes of All Saint's and St Mary's shall amalgamate, and provide a suitable cemetery. The Board will select the most convenient spot, and the expenses of the whole are to be defrayed in proportion to the assessment of each parish, viz.: St Mary's to pay seven elevenths, and All Saints four elevenths.

28th March 1857

Newmarket – *Mysterious Disappearance* – Last week Mr Thomas Cole, clerk to Mr Tyrell Moody, brewer, of this town, suddenly left the town under circumstances at present unexplained. His absence has been a source of considerable uneasiness to his family, and great inconvenience to the business, of which he had the principle management, and the entire confidence of his employer, and being unmarried, and possessed of some property, and in nowise addicted to either drinking or gambling, and his accounts having not as yet been pronounced deficient, no reason has been assigned for his leaving the town, in which he was much respected, so abruptly. It appears that some gentlemen in the town, have had one or two letters from him, but not the slightest clue to his whereabouts has yet transpired.

11th April 1857

The Election – Great excitement prevailed in this little metropolis of the sporting world on Friday last. The polling commenced at eight o'clock and continued briskly till after two in the afternoon. The Tories had their committee room next door to the Jockey Club Rooms, formally occupied by the Bench of Magistrates. On Tuesdays it is also used as a committee room for the Jockey Club. The liberals occupied a committee room next door to the Rutland Arms and only a short distance from the polling place, the latter being held at the Literary Institution Reading rooms. The Liberals kept very quiet, and did not issue any statement of the poll for the first few hours, but the Tories kept issuing them at intervals, but their statements did not agree with the statement of the Liberals by a great many votes; however, it will be seen at the close of the poll that Mr Adeane's committee were much nearer the mark than the other all the way through. At the close of the poll the Liberals had their statement posted up before the Tories received their telegraphic message and they (the Liberals) appeared to manage it extremely well, particularly when the 'young-un' began to take the lead of Lord George Manners.
The Court for both Suffolk and Cambridge sessions was by now held in the new Police Court and Station. Built in 1856 it still stands opposite the Carpenters Arms in All Saints Road, although now in private hands.

16th May 1857

Newmarket – *Painful Disclosures* – It is with much pain we announce that disclosures of a most astounding character have been made during the past few days, in reference to the management of the estate of the Duke of Rutland, at Cheveley. Deficiencies and irregularities, extending over a series of years, have been discovered, by which it is feared the noble owner will be a considerable loser. The agent alluded to has left this part of the country. It is needless to say that the rumour has caused the deepest sensation in Newmarket and the neighbourhood.

Railway Station – For a considerable time the public were subjected to great inconvenience at the station, in consequence of the crowded condition of the platform; and the farmers and merchants complained that their men and teams were detained for many hours when sent with or for loads of corn and goods. Corn and parcels of almost every description were indiscriminately piled together upon the platform, a system which created great confusion and danger, as the platform is laid over very deep cellars, and a few months since it broke in while the porters were removing a cask of sugar, and crushed the leg of one of them, from the effects of which he has not yet recovered. Since this accident, the Company have erected a commodious goods station, and proper arrangements have been made for the comfort of passengers, and to facilitate the loading and unloading of corn, etc.

8th August 1857

Saint Mary's Church – Some time since a scheme was projected for the enlargement of this church, which is highly necessary in a town like Newmarket, with an increasing population, but from some cause or other it could not be carried out notwithstanding the exertions of the late Incumbent and other respectable families of the town. However the parishioners of St Mary's are not altogether unmindful of their church. And although there is no existing probability of its being enlarged it is now undergoing a through alteration and repair. The whole of the interior has been taken out and the worn out floor removed, and the beautiful and comfortable modern benches are to be substituted for the heavy box pews, the floor boarded, and everything done for the improvement of the fabric as well as for the comfort of the congregation. The churchyard is also undergoing a change, and a good paved drain has been made completely round the exterior of the church and other parts of the yard. Gas will be laid into the church. While this church is under repair extra services are held in All Saint's Church.

19th September 1857

Fatal Accident – During the afternoon of Tuesday, 15th instant, Mr Edward Haylock, bricklayer, of Newmarket, fell from a scaffold, erected in the front of the Wellington Inn, about half past two o'clock, into the street; he was immediately taken home, and medical attendance procured, but he did not survive two hours. He regained his facilities, and stated that, having ascended the scaffold, he, in stepping back, trod on the handle of a *hawk*, and was precipitated to the ground. He also requested his man to fetch his tools from the Wellington, and deposit them in a certain shed, and give the keys to his mistress. The man did so, and went up stairs and told him he had done so, when he said it was "all right" and shortly afterwards expired. An inquest was held on the body on Wednesday,

before J M Peck, Esq., deputy coroner, and a verdict of 'Accidental Death' returned. It was stated that an intimate friend of the deceased, Mr Christopher Wakefield, jockey, was killed riding a race at Bridgewater on the same day, and about the same hour.

17th October 1857

Accident – Yesterday week, as a man named Henry Swan was driving his horse and cart through the High Street, Newmarket, the horse became unmanageable, and ran upon the footpath between a pile of boxes and the shop of Mr Andrews, and knocked down the wife and child of C Hammond, Esq., of the Bank. We are sorry to report that when Mrs Hammond and her child had been with difficulty extricated from their perilous position it was found that the former had sustained a fracture of the leg. She is, however, doing well. The child happily escaped unhurt.
Fuller Andrews, shopkeeper, High Street. White 1855

30th October 1857

State of the Town – Newmarket has been for some time looking down, now, we are happy to state, things are very decidedly on the mend. During the past few weeks, several large racing establishments have been taken by gentlemen; and others, we understand are being inquired for. The enormous rents demanded for private houses, we think injure the town more than anything else. But rents have fallen much, and must fall still more.

The Great Pig Case – Much amusement has been excited during this past week in racing and other circles, at Newmarket, by a dispute about a pig, between two well known persons; and it is reported that the affair is likely to give rise to some litigation. Some facetious friend circulated lithographic likenesses of the animal, with a large carrot in his mouth; the great bone of contention being the quantity of carrots possible to be consumed by a pig in a given time. Perhaps some of our readers, who put out or take in pigs to joist, can determine the question. In the event of litigation, it will be the old case of the oyster, or even worse, for the lawyers will swallow pig, skin and all. *Correspondent.*

31st October 1857

Finding a Bank note – On Saturday last, as David Hum, the town scavenger, was sweeping the street, he found a roll of bank notes amounting to £150. Having been cried, he took them to the owner, and was rewarded with £5.

7th November 1857

Re-opening of St Mary's Church – The church was re-opened on Sunday last, when service was performed in the morning and evening, and the Rev Plumpton Wilson, some years since the rector of the parish, was invited to preach the opening sermons. For a considerable time before service, the church was thronged by persons anxious to obtain a seat, and on the doors being opened, was quickly filled. The Rev gentlemen preached an appropriate and excellent sermon from 2 Cor. V. 17,18. In the evening, the church was filled long before the hour appointed for service, and at the commencement of the prayers even standing room could not be found in the church. The windows were taken possession of by scores, the porches crammed with attentive listeners, and hundreds were unable to obtain admittance, and contented themselves in the churchyard, eager to catch one word from their former worthy minister. The Rev gentleman delivered an affecting and impressive discourse from Exodus xx. 24 and eloquently pointed out the value of a temple of worship in the midst of a people, The prayers were read by the Rev James Isaacson, the present rector, and the Rev John Taylor, late incumbent of All Saints, also assisted the service. Collections were made both morning and evening to £ 11 5s 2d. The organ was played in a masterly style by Mr C Frye, jun., and the choir sang with effect a hymn, composed for the occasion by C Hammond, Esq.

21st November 1857

Burial Board – A letter has been received from the Secretary of State requesting further explanation of the objections raised by the vestry of All Saints, to the proposed site for the new burial ground. One would have thought the resolutions passed were quite explicit enough. The approach is through the narrow Wellington Lane already much to narrow for the traffic, and liable to be blocked up as it frequently is by the most trifling occurrence, across the Mill Hill where the fair is held, through a second narrow gauge, bounded by rows of the very poorest cottages in the town, the road in front of which is made the receptacle of all filth imaginable. And then the road past the Union house is one of the bleakest round Newmarket, exposed to all the northern winds, without a shadow of protection. The whole aspect of the ground at once shows that a bleaker and more unsuitable spot could not have been selected, and in event of its approval we pity those whose duties may compel their attendance on a bitter wintry day in such an inhospitable spot. Moreover, with the site generally approved of by the inhabitants, near the railway station, the use of hearses and horses might be dispensed with for at least two-thirds of the funerals, but this is the real cause of the opposition to it. The price asked for the land, £200 per acre, is preposterous, the actual value being about £60 per acre. With a rackrent, assessment, and rates seven and eight shillings in the pound, we think it madness to pursue a course which can only end in an addition of an annual rate of two to three shillings in the pound to our heavy burdens. With high rents, enormous taxes, sanitary or *insanitary* rates, of nearly two shillings in the pound, we ought to advocate economy rather than lavish expenditure, and property is depreciating in value daily in the town of Newmarket. No wonder, therefore, that some persons do all they can to get rid of their property. We do hope the inhabitants will rouse themselves and generally petition the Secretary of State. – *Correspondent.*

When the graveyards associated with the two parish churches of St Mary's and All Saints became full, the vestries had to find land for a new graveyard. Two possible sites were identified one near the Union Workhouse and the other by the Railway Station. The newspaper was reporting almost every week about the controversy that raged in the town over this issue. (See September 1858). This report is of further interest as it describes conditions in Newmarket town centre in the 1850's and what a bleak situation the Union Workhouse must have stood in half way between Newmarket and Exning.

21st November 1857

Death by a Kick by a Horse – On Sunday the 9th inst., a man named Robert Marshal, many years postlad at the Rutland Arms, in this town was kicked on the thigh by a horse, from the injuries of which he died on Saturday last, leaving a wife and family.

1858

9th January 1858

Re Messrs Bryant – Some degree of sympathy is manifested in this town and neighbourhood for the unfortunate position of the affairs of the Messrs Bryant. Some parties were uncharitable enough to think that the insolvency was occasioned by a want of due precaution, and that the evil day was approaching with out an attempt to avert the consequences, but it now appears that the prevailing opinion of the public is that Mr R Bryant has endeavoured to act in reality throughout in an honourable and business like manner. When the estate devolved upon them they unexpectedly found it involved in pecuniary difficulties, and at once formed a resolution to surmount them, and by exertions in business and economical management, thought to clear off the whole, but not withstanding their united endeavours failed. The suspension of their business was occasioned by the non–payment of a Government debt of £4462 1s 4d to the Excise for malt duty, and for which he was arrested, and the property placed in bond. On Saturday last two juries were empanelled and inquisitions held in the County Court at the White Hart inn, Newmarket, under a Writ of Extent, before the Undersheriffs of the Counties of Cambridge and Suffolk, for the purpose of ascertaining the amount of their personal property, etc. Evidence was given of the value of various portions of their estate, which in Suffolk was stated as upwards of £7000, upon which the Crown has a priority of claim, and as the Crown holds the property, the Excise debt will be discharged, and the residue revert to the estate for the creditors. The book debts were about £200, and the stock of Malt in hand laid at about 1,200 qrs. We are requested by the officers of Excise to remove the opinion that the arrest was an act of cruelty. The Supervisor informed us that the Writ was issued in the usual way, and authorised an arrest, and was put into the hands of the Sheriff, with an intimation not to arrest, or defer it, but as the writ ordered an arrest the Sheriff considered a verbal request not to arrest, insufficient, and accordingly the Sheriff not the Excise, acted upon the authority of the writ. It is supposed that as soon as matters are settled, Messrs Bryants will resume business.

23rd January 1858

The death of Mr Tyrell Moody, brewer.

30th January 1858

Accident – As Mr Wm. Hitchin, landlord of the Horse Shoes Inn, was twisting himself round upon one leg on Wednesday last. He unfortunately broke his leg.

6th February 1858

Narrow Escape – *Caution in Handling Guns* – Amongst the collection of articles for auction in the public street, on Tuesday last, was a gun, which several had curiosity to inspect, and one person put a cap upon the nipple, and was holding it in a pointing direction up the street, with the intention of striking it off as a test not knowing it was loaded, but fortunately on pulling the trigger he turned the muzzle towards the Palace wall, and to the surprise of every one the gun went off, the charge striking the wall with terrific violence, and cutting a considerable dent in the brickwork, and cutting of the lock of a cupboard standing near; the shot rebounded from the wall in many directions and struck several bystanders, one or two of which were wounded in the face.

20th February 1858

The Crown Inn – Bartholomew, the well known jockey, having given up his turf engagements and taken the Crown Inn, in this place, a large party assembled on Friday last to partake of his opening dinner, no less than forty five gentlemen having taken tickets. Everything passed off satisfactorily, and the company dispersed at a late hour.
James Bartholomew, Crown, High Street. PO Directory 1864. The Crown Inn, shown on John Chapman's map of 1787, dates back to at least 1577. In a 1617 will, it was recorded as having a Butt (108 gallons), a Pipe (36 gallons), and 21 Hogsheads (54 gallons each) of beer.

6th March 1858

The Weather – For the last nine or ten days in February, the weather was very cold, with piecing easterly winds, and some apprehension is entertained for the condition of the wheat crops; and agricultural operations have been entirely suspended. March, as every one knows, was introduced in a very cold and unpleasant manner, in accordance with the ancient adage, 'He came in like a lion, and we hope, will go out like a lamb' – the genuine March breeze on

Monday morning being increased in severity to that of the last few days, and the heavy appearance of the atmosphere presaged an early downfall, which set in heavily during the afternoon. The fall of snow throughout the night was considerable, and on Tuesday was so drifted from the exposed lands, that every valley and partially sheltered place, and many public roads, for many miles around Newmarket, were completely blocked up, and in some instances were altogether impassable. The scanty attendance at market was the result of the condition of the roads, and those who were present boasted that they had reached market through great exertions, by travelling over fields, or other wise out-of-the-way routes, and it was really amusing to hear those who had driven through the snow-drifts wondering how they could manage to get home, and some even doubting the possibility. On Wednesday morning, the mail to Newmarket was between three and four hours behind the time, and the country delivery was about three hours late, for in addition to the delay of the bags by mail, the country messengers were obliged to proceed over land tracts and by-ways some distance from their accustomed roads. In several hollow situated roads, the snow is lying from one to six feet deep, and are being cleared by cutting.

13th March 1858

The Rutland Memorial - When it was first suggested that some suitable object should be raised by public subscription in memory of the late Duke of Rutland, the majority of those living in the neighbourhood of Newmarket were strongly in favour of a statue, which at one time it was thought would be erected, but the Committee appointed for the proper management of any adopted scheme very wisely determined to recommend a scheme which would not only be worthy to be considered a fit memento of so good and great a person as the late Duke, but at the same time would be useful and ornamental, and it was finally resolved that a parsonage house should be erected in and for the extremely poor living of Newmarket All Saints parish. Although this resolution was carried by a majority at a public meeting, several of the public expressed dissatisfaction, and openly refused to contribute what they had promised or intended. However, the gentlemen entrusted with the carrying out of the memorial were not discouraged, and eventually, after more mature consideration, subscriptions were more

liberally sent in, and several who had contributed most cheerfully increased the amount they had first given under the scheme for a statue. The subscription list amounts at present to about £900, and other sums will continue to be sent in. According to the plan of the intended building, it will have a very pretty appearance, the front consisting or two tower sides, and the centre formed by a large and well designed tablet, bearing an inscription to the memory of his Grace, the late Duke, surmounted by a fine monumental tower or spire. His Grace, the present Duke, has expressed a cordial approval of the plan, knowing that such a residence was really essential, and that it is really what would have been most gratifying to his late beloved father. A meeting of the Committee has been held respecting the site upon which the house is to be built, and the necessary arrangement are being made for the commencement of the works. *This memorial was for John Henry Manners 5th Duke of Rutland born 1778 died 1857. During the Duke's widowhood 1825-1857 he hardly ever lived at Cheveley Park, but lodged at the former royal palace in Newmarket.*

24th April 1858

Railway Carelessness - The two p.m. train on Monday last had coupled to it a horse box, in which was a race-horse and a boy. A porter to save trouble, attempted to double shunt; the train backed out of the Station, and the man held the points until the horse-box was clear, when he let go the handle and the train ran straight on, but unfortunately he forgot the most particular part of the performance, namely the uncoupling the horse-box from the train, and the result was as the train was passing it dragged the horse-box over on its side, the little boy got out of the window, frightened very much but the horse could not be got out so easily, he kicked and struggled very much, and was not got out till the box was righted again; he was not much injured, and is said to be Mr Barnard's horse Good Friday. The porter has been called up to London to answer for his conduct.

Burial Board – The two parishes of St Mary's and All Saints are still divided in their choice of ground for the contemplated cemetery and nothing like mutuality in the matter is probable. The burying grounds are inconveniently full, and unless a site is agreed upon before the end of next month the Government will have to select for them.

The Union Flour ~ Numerous complaints have been made of the quality of the flour supplied to the paupers in this union, and upon inquiry it was discovered that the complaints were not without cause. It appears that the contractor in his tender presented a very good sample of flour which was consequently accepted, and one or two samples were in accordance with the contract, but some of the very worst qualities have since been sent out amongst the paupers who find a repeated allowance of inferior flour, which could hardly be worked into bread, very properly made complaints in the proper quarter. We understand that the Board of Guardians have investigated the matter, and it is to be hoped will take proper steps to protect the poor as well as ratepayers.

8th May 1858

Tom Matthews ~ This celebrated clown gave two entertainments in the Public-hall, in this town, on Monday and Tuesday last, and was well patronised. His songs were very good of the sort, and his tricks, peculiar to a public clown, and quaint sayings, could not fail to excite the risible muscles, and much fun and laughter were the result. Miss Matthews assisted in the entertainment by presiding at the pianoforte, and gave satisfaction to her audience.

22nd May 1858

Nuisance ~ Great complaint is made of the effluvium arising from the repository of rags, bones and skins, of slaughtered animals at the corner of All Saints Church, which is very sickening and disagreeable to the inhabitants and visitors of this part of the town. It is hoped that the public complaints will not be unheeded, and that the authorities will have it removed as soon as convenient.

12th June 1858

The Audience at one Place, the Performers at Another – Last week, bills and placards were posted in this town and vicinity, announcing a grand performance by 'Christy's American Minstrels' on Wednesday evening, and at the appointed time many paid their money and took their seats, but after they waited some time, it was discovered that no such performers were in the town, and the company left without any entertainment, at least to themselves. This was not all, for it turned out that bills had been ordered to announce the performance at Needham Market, but by some mistake, were printed for Newmarket, and as no bills were issued for Needham Market, the Minstrels were in attendance at that place without an audience, whilst an audience had assembled at Newmarket without performers.

Singers and musician blacking their faces and performing Minstrel music came into its own in 1843 with the formation of The Virginia Minstrels in America they were followed closely by Ed Christy's Minstrels.

12th June 1858

The Tempest ~ A very heavy tempest passed over this town and neighbourhood on Saturday morning last, and continued more or less severe throughout the day. The thunder was terrific, and the lighting forked and vivid, and the rain descended in torrents, accompanied by violent winds. The electric fluid struck a chimney in New Town, a short distance from the railway station, completely splitting it in twain from the top to the bottom, broke through the gable end of the house, and struck the woman while in the act of pouring water from the kettle to the teapot, and then passed out at the door with tremendous crash. The woman had a very narrow escape, being scorched, and her arm so much injured that it was thought she would not recover the use of it. Several other accidents were caused by the tempest, but we have not as yet heard of anything serious.

19th June 1858

Dibbling Machines – Mr Charles Clarke, the master of the Newmarket Union, has invented a very useful and convenient dibbling machine. The dibbles work on a rotary principle, and having a second and independent movement of their own; for, having punctured the ground in their revolution the dibs are drawn out and a perfect hole remains, effected by the revolution on their own axis. This instrument can be used for every kind of seed, and is certainly superior to anything yet invented for similar work. Several of the most practical agriculturists of the country have tested this machine, and highly approve of its principle.

19th June 1858

The Horticultural Society – This Society is making rapid progress. The Committee have just announced their First Grand Musical and

Horticultural Fete for Friday, the 9th July next, in the Park Grounds of William Parr Isaacson, Esq., under the patronage of the most distinguished persons when, by permission of Col. Key, the band of the 15th Hussars will be in attendance, and during the afternoon, play popular airs and overtures. The grounds will be open at 2 o'clock, and close at 8. Admission up to 4 o'clock will be 2s and from that time 1s. There will be refreshments on the grounds at the usual charges, and the prize list and conditions for competitors can be obtained on application to the Secretaries. Members are allowed three free tickets.

Willoughby House stood next to the Jockey Club on the site of the present Post Office. It was purchased by William Parr Isaacson from William Crockford in 1844. He eventually bought the next property, Panton House, described as having an extensive pleasure garden, a kitchen garden, stables, outhouses, etc.

4th September 1858

Burial Board – All difficulties and misunderstanding existing respecting the choice of ground for the new Cemetery are at last surmounted by the unanimous approval of a field opposite the White Lion belonging to the Duke of Rutland, which the Board had obtained an offer of, and recommended to the parishioners. At vestry meetings of the two parishes, on Thursday week, it was unanimously agreed that £400 be given for the ground, and £100 to the widow of Mr Westey, as a compensation for the non-purchase of the ground first bargained for of her late husband, and every arrangement was made for the commencement of the building and laying out the ground. Contracts are advertised for and plans prepared so that the work may proceed without unnecessary delay. According to the plan, the ground will be divided, and two chapels erected for the Church people and Dissenters – the buildings to be detached in body, but connected above by a span or arch, upon which the funeral bell will be suspended. The selection and purchase of this ground is approved of by the whole town, and is happily the means of uniting the two parishes, and of removing the previous differences of opinion on this matter.

The layout of the cemetery, chapels, lodge, walling, and entrance were the work of local architect, John Francis Clark. Mr Westey's land was next to the Union Workhouse on Exning Road.

4th September 1858

The Turf – Wasting – A few days since, as Mr Garrod, of Cheveley-park, was driving to Newmarket, he found Sam Rogers, the well-known jockey, lying upon the road quite exhausted from severe wasting, and in a very faint condition. Mr Rogers' friend was standing by him and begged that Mr Garrod would convey him home; and accordingly he was assisted into the cart, and driven home accordingly. Too great exertion in wasting for riding is frequently indulged in, and unless great care is exercised it results fatally and invariably brings on apoplexy.

Wasting was a method of weight control used by racing jockeys. A mixture of starving and turkish baths, with a road run to rapidly reduce the body weight before a race. The sweat room used by Fred Archer is still in existence at Heath House stables in Newmarket. Siltzer in his book, sites Dullingham Road as a favourite for this purpose, as it was enclosed by high hedges and therefore adapted to keeping the wind from a pedestrian and inducing perspiration. Samuel Rogers, horse trainer and jockey, High Street. PO Directory 1864

28th October 1858

Sudden Death – On Saturday evening last, a little boy named John Thomas Choat, eight years of age, son of Mr John Choat, baker of this town dropped down dead upon the Exning Road. The deceased had been to the mill with his brothers and sisters and fell down while they were looking into a field. Seeing him lying behind them they returned, called and shook him, and thinking he had fainted, tried to put him into the bakers basket which they had with them. Failing to do so they ran off to the town to give information, but in the interval the deceased was found by the man at the gas house. He was conveyed to the Union and put into a warm bath, but life was extinct. It is said that the deceased had been a sickly child, but was much improved during the last twelve months.

13th November 1858

Betting – its Reverses and End – The Field, a sporting paper, has the following:- Mr Robert Ridsdale died suddenly at Newmarket on Sunday last. He had been a turf character of some celebrity in former years, but a sad reverse of fortune had reduced him to a state of poverty, almost destitution. He won the Derby 1832, with

St Giles, when he received on the day of settling no less a sum than £46000. He had also a share in Bloomsbury, the winner of the Derby in 1839; but his means at that time were not sufficient to enable him to win a large sum. He had at one time (about twenty-five years ago) nearly 200 horses eating hay and corn on his estate, Murton, near York. Now alas! he was buried by subscription.

Mr Ridsdale won the Derby with St Giles in 1832, in partnership with the pugilist Gully (see 17th October 1807) however a disagreement about bets dissolved the alliance. Silzer.

4th December 1858

Harwood House – We some times since gave an account of the good intentions of Mr J Smith the occupier of this house, by forming a portion of his dwelling into a chapel, and holding religious services for the instruction of the poor, and those of the town who never thought of attending a place of worship. He has now a very numerous congregation regularly attending his house.

1859

1st January 1859

Christmas Holiday – Christmas was observed in this town and district with a genuine national spirit, and while preparations were being made by the more wealthy of our neighbours, the poor families were by no means forgotten. In Newmarket a free distribution of bread, meat, and other necessities was made to all the poor people of the town; and the inmates of the Union were supplied with a bountiful repast of Christmas comforts, plum puddings, roast beef, tea, beer, tobacco, etc.; and all enjoyed themselves to their hearts content. In the surrounding villages, the labouring classes were cared for by their employers, and received presents of meat and money, so that not a cottage was without a good joint and other seasonable food on Christmas day.

15th January 1859

Invitation Balls – On Thursday night week, an invitation ball took place in the Public Hall, under the management of a Committee of the Literary Institute, and was attended by between 90 and 100 of the farmers, tradesmen, and others of the town and neighbourhood. An excellent quadrille band was engaged from Cambridge,

and dancing was kept up till about five o'clock in the morning. Refreshments and wines were supplied by the Rutland Arms Company, and were tastefully arranged in the Reading rooms of the hall, and all appeared to enjoy the evening's entertainment. A juvenile ball by invitation, was held in the hall on the following night, when about fifty young persons danced to the enlivening music of the same band till midnight.

Sam Cowell's Concert – On Thursday week our Public Hall was filled by an audience attracted thither by the fame of Sam Cowell, who elicited his inimitable ministrations of buffo songs such genuine and ringing laughter that the walls re-echoed with the sound, and his auditors were literally moved to tears of mirth. But '*place aux dames*' Miss Henry, a pleasing soprano was admirably seconded by her sister Miss Mary Henry, and their united voices harmonised well with the fine baritone of Mr Frederick Gough, who was most successful in the songs allotted to him, Mr James Hicks presided ably at the piano, and the concertina, by his masterly touch, became a many voiced instrument. Mr Sam Cowell introduced himself to the audience in his own extravaganza, 'Alonzo the Brave and the fair Imogene', and his rapid changes from grave to gay, from lively to severe, were most ludicrous.

Sam Cowell [1822-66] was the star performer at Evans's Supper Rooms in Covent Garden, London, the forerunner of the Victorian music hall. He came from a professional acting family. His father had been a popular actor in America, where Sam began his own career. His most famous song was 'The Ratcatcher's Daughter'.

15th January 1859

Narrow Escape – On Thursday week some men, employed by Mr Hitchen, in Newmarket were engaged in sinking or clearing out a well, upwards of 60 feet deep, when the young man working below called out to those above to draw him up. One of the drawers was away at the time, and the other left to call him, and in the mean time the man in the well pulled the rope, which caused the roller to revolve with great rapidity till the rope was unwound, when the sudden jerk dislodged the roller from the frame, which fell with a tremendous force to the bottom of the well. Fortunately the roller, which was a heavy one, pitched upon its end on the opposite side of the well to which the man was standing otherwise he must be crushed to death. One of the winchers struck the poor man upon the back part of his head and inflicted an extensive and serious wound, but assistance and medical aid was quickly rendered, and we hope the man is in a fair way of recovery.

Oliver Hitchen, bricklayer, Albion Street. White 1855

Telegraphs – The posts for the telegraph from Norwich to London have been erected as far as Newmarket for several weeks past, but some difficulty appears to have arisen in passing the town, as strong objections have been made to placing the posts, which would doubtless be a source of considerable inconvenience. We have not yet heard how the wires are to be conveyed through the town, but it is supposed that they will be carried underground.

This report refers to The Electric Telegraph Company that was merged with the International Telegraph Company in 1853 to become The Electric & International Telegraph Co. They provided the signalling systems for the railways in East Anglia before entering into road line construction, eventually the Post Office took over the private companies in 1870.

22nd January 1859

A Take in Lecture – Last week, a person calling himself Dr Welch, visited this town, and obtained permission to deliver a lecture in the National Schoolroom, on Thursday evening. He called upon the Rev J Isaacson, rector of St Mary's to whom he presented a few testimonials purporting to be written by the Rev E Pellew, of Bury St Edmunds, and other clergymen. Having succeeded in obtaining a quantity of printed bills, in which he attempted to gull the public by a statement that he had already been honoured by the patronage of some of the most respectable families of the town and neighbourhood, he called at the principle houses to dispose of his cards, and to induce parties to purchase them made use of a forged recommendation of the Rev J Isaacson. As soon as this was made known, his sale of tickets ceased, and many of those who held them refused to attend the lecture, plausibly described upon his bills as an instructive description of the manners and customs of the American Indians. At the time appointed about 25 persons were present, some of whom went merely out of curiosity, and the lecture is represented as one of the most miserable attempts remembered. (The good people of Ely were served in a similar manner, by the same person, last week. – Ed.)

Harwood House – Lecture – On Friday evening last, a very instructive and able lecture on 'Iron, and its Qualities' was delivered, gratuitously, at the Chapel-room, at Harwood House, by Mr H A Long, of Cambridge. The company was unusually numerous, and consisted of the working classes, and those of the religious society under the ministry of the Rev J Smith, who at the termination of the lecture, read the anniversary report of the institution, which was adopted in the heartiest manner, with the best wishes of the meeting for the increased success of Mr Smith's efforts.

Raffle – A Valuable horse and pony, belonging to Mr P Munnings, Cheveley, were put up at the White Hart Inn, Newmarket, on Tuesday evening last. The conditions were that the highest number should win the horse, and the lowest should claim the pony, and, singularly enough, both were won by the putter up, who raffled for two absent members.

29th January 1859

Public Hall – Sinclair's Panorama of Russia and India, has been here for the last three days and has attracted large audiences. The scenes are painted on canvas in a superior manner, and those of India are really excellent. The entertainment is enlivened by Mr Newman, who delivers a brief but comprehensive lecture, and also sings appropriate songs in a very effective manner; whilst Master Fitzgerald, 'The Modern Tom Thumb' who is 17 years old, stands only 35 inches in height and weighs only 36 pounds, amused the audience with his drollies etc., etc.; in fact he may be considered next to the 'General Tom Thumb'; and as the admission is very reasonable, we recommend every one who has the chance to pay a visit.

26th February 1859

Lecture – A lecture on 'Circumstantial Evidence' was delivered at the Public Hall, on Tuesday evening last. There was a large audience, many of whom took a deep interest in the subject.

Ventriloquism – The celebrated ventriloquist, Mr Newman, has been giving very clever and amusing entertainments at the Schools in the villages in the Newmarket district, during the last fortnight. His power as a ventriloquist is certainly remarkable, and has given unlimited satisfaction, and must be heard to be appreciated. Mrs and Miss Newman greatly improved the entertainment by their vocal performance.

26th February 1859

Insolvent ~ At the Insolvent Court, London, on Wednesday last, Eliza Paris, formerly of Newmarket, came up for hearing, she was opposed by Mr Reed for a number of creditors, and supported by Mr Sargood. It appeared that the insolvent was the widow of the late Arthur Paris, the well-known Newmarket jockey. Sir Robert Peel was inserted as a debtor, and marked 'doubtful', which meant that he disputed the debt for the occupancy of the house at Newmarket. The house was mortgaged, but had cost a considerable sum beyond the money raised. She came away from Newmarket, and resided with Mr Slate, at Paddington, one of the opposing creditors. Other creditors at Newmarket opposed. A letter was read from Sir Robert Peel denying his liability, as he was deprived of the tenancy during Spring Meeting. The Court named a day for the final order and required further information. The protection was renewed.

Paris is probably a misprint for Parvis. Arthur Parvis first raced at Exeter in 1821. He was happily married and had a charming home at Newmarket, adorned with every comfort of the day and completed by a fine collection of sporting prints and pictures of race horses. His house stood somewhere between the White Hart and Black Bear Lane and was described in 1842 as looking 'like a villa come down on a week's visit from Cheltenham or St Leonards. He died after a short illness of only two days on 15th October 1839. Silzer

5th March 1859

Electric Telegraph – It is now decided that the wires of the telegraph from Norwich to London are to be carried through this town in pipes under the main street, for some considerable distance upon the London and Bury turnpikes, and about sixty labourers are employed in making the tunnel for that purpose. Several of the posts have been removed from the east entrance of the town as far as the exercising heath extends, in consequence of the noise from the wires etc., being objected to by owners and trainers of race horses.

12th March 1859

The Electric Telegraph – The wires of the road telegraph from Norwich to London were laid through the main street of the town, and nearly a mile at each end from the town, in about three days of last week. There are seven small wires, enclosed in a gutta-percha case, and then carefully turned over each other in the form of a rope, and the whole encased in a gutta-percha tube, not larger than common bowl of a tobacco pipe, with a coat of tarred tow, and finally deposited in a wooden case, about a foot and a half from the surface. The wires were frequently tested, and found to communicate freely with the centre of the town to Norwich, but since the conclusion of the subterranean work, we understand that some defect has been found in one of the wires, which is now being remedied.

Gutta Percha is a resin from the Isonandra Gutta Tree. The milky fluid is evaporated to produce a material that softens in hot water and has the advantage of becoming hard without being brittle and has good waterproofing and insulating properties.

26th March 1859

Marine Store Nuisance ~ There are two rag and bone yards in All Saints parish, which are a perfect nuisance to that part of the town. The case has been laid before the Local Board of Health, and we hope the grievance will be speedily remedied.

New Dibbling Machine – Mr Clarke, Master of the Newmarket Union, has received a Letters Patent for the invention of improvements in machinery for dibbling wheat and other grain and manure. The invention and perfecting of the machine cost Mr Clarke a considerable amount of time and money, and reflects great credit to him. Many gentlemen and practical men have examined and tested this machine, and declare it to be the best and most useful implement for such purposes yet invented. Numerous orders have reached Mr Clarke from various parts of the country, and it is supposed that in many instances it will supersede the drill.

2nd April 1859

Newmarket – *The Union* – We are happy to report that the Board of Guardians of this district are at this time in a position to lighten the burden of the rate payers of the district by calls of considerably less sums for the Union expenses. We understand that the call upon the district is something like £3000 below that of the former levy. This decrease in the expenditure of the Union is attributed to the cheapness of the necessaries of life, and the satisfactory condition of the working classes.

Harwood House – On Thursday last, an interesting lecture upon 'George Stephenson', was delivered at Harwood Assembly Rooms, by the Rev George Irving Hitchin, of Brandon. The meeting, which was very numerous, chiefly of the working classes, was presided over by G B Mead, Esq.
George Borwick Mead MD, surgeon and medical referee to National Provincial Life Assurance, High Street. PO Directory 1864

The Marine Store Nuisance – These receptacles of the skins and bones of animals, reported last week, have been visited by Drs. Page and Day, and pronounced to be disgusting places, and very injurious to health. Certificates to this effect have been sent to Mr Jarrold, to produce before the Board of Health, who will immediately proceed against the proprietors of these buildings, unless the nuisances complained of are abated.

9th April 1859

Window Breaking – Between one and two o'clock on Saturday morning, a fellow, wandering in the front street of this town, called at the house occupied by the Rev Mr Knipe, and demanded admittance and lodgings, and on being remonstrated with, proceeded to smash the window of the sitting room. He was taken before the Magistrate on the following morning and committed to Bury Goal for one month.

30th April 1859

Electric Telegraph – An office is now being fitted up at the Post Office, in the centre of this town, in connection with the underground telegraph, and we understand that similar ones are in contemplation for other towns along the new line.
Extract from the Electric & International Telegraph Company's scale of charges, January 1863. Newmarket. Telegraphic code NR. Hours of opening, Weekday 8 am - 8 pm. Sunday 8 am - 8 pm. Office opposite Betting Rooms. High Street. Open to 11 pm during races. Wires extended to race course, office only open one hour before first race and until one hour after last, each day. BT Archive Post 81/44. The 1861 census for St Mary's, Newmarket, records the Telegraph Office at the above site (for Post Office, see Aug 1856). Bearing in mind the difficulties involved in moving any telegraph cables once installed. I would think it was quite possible that the Post Office moved across the road into the Telegraph Office when the General Post Office took over the control of the telegraph system in 1870, remaining there until the building was destroyed by a bomb in World War II. (See March 1860)

The Rutland Arms

21st May 1859

Rutland Hotel – It will be seen by the *London Gazette* of May 6, that the 'Rutland Hotel Company', formed for the purpose of preventing this Hotel being closed until a proper person could be found to enter upon it, has been dissolved, and that Mr Thos. Bacon, the late manager of the Ship Hotel, Greenwich, is now sole lessee under his Grace the Duke of Rutland. A hope is entertained that under Mr Bacon's able management, much improvement may be effected, his assiduity and attention to his guests during the late 'meeting' having been given very general satisfaction.

18th June 1859

Presentation of the Rutland Memorial to the Living of All Saints Parish. – The new parsonage house for the parish of All Saints, in this town, erected by voluntary subscription, in memory of the late Duke of Rutland, is now completed, and will shortly be occupied by the incumbent. This building is pleasantly situated at the S.E. entrance of the town, and is a combination of monumental ornament and domestic convenience, and a suitable memorial of that great and benevolent nobleman whose fame and liberality it is designed to perpetrate. The period for giving the incumbent possession of the house having arrived was suggested, and unanimously agreed by the committee, that his Grace the Duke of Rutland should be invited to receive the memorial at their hands, in order to present it to the representative of the living of All Saints, and his Grace having been pleased to accept the invitation of the subscribers, Saturday last was appointed for the presentation ceremony. His Grace arrived by the eleven o'clock train from London and was met by a body of the principle subscribers, the clergy and gentlemen of the town and neighbourhood, the church bells of All Saints ringing merrily to welcome him, and at once proceeded to the memorial house. Having inspected the interior and grounds surrounding the building his Grace was met upon the lawn by the subscribers, where the Rev E Mortlock of Moulton, in the name of the subscribers generally, presented to his Grace the key and possession of the house. The rev. gentlemen, having briefly adverted to the original schemes for the erection of a suitable monument in memory of the late Duke, and the reason for erecting the present one, assured his Grace that they were all mindful of the kindness of disposition of his Grace's noble parent, and that they had in this design endeavoured to imitate his greatness. He trusted that his Grace would be of opinion that the architect, who liberally contributed the design, had fully accomplished their desires.

All Saints Vicarage

Having received the key, the noble Duke, who appeared much affected, in reply, said. "Mr Mortlock and gentlemen, I am indeed deeply grateful to you on this occasion in fact I cannot find words sufficient to thank you for your kindness in presenting so excellent a memorial of my beloved father and my difficulty is enhanced in this duty today in consequence of its being of a mixed and tender character, I assure you that every day, nay, almost every hour, I feel most keenly the loss of that beloved parent, and on an occasion like this present everything relating to him is recalled more vividly to my recollection. Although his presence is no longer with us, and although we no longer have him amongst us to aid and guide us by his counsels, and to make our homes happy, yet the recollections of his virtues are engraven, as this important ceremony today evinces, deeply and indelibly in our hearts and minds. I am truly thankful to you, gentlemen, for your expression of respect to my beloved father in the erection of this memorial, and beg to say that, in my opinion, the decision you came to was the wisest and the best that could have been devised. I think there is no monument you could have raised to his memory that would have been more in accordance with and pleasing to his feelings than the one you have now erected, and if he had had the opportunity to express his opinion thereon, he would have preferred it to any other, for he was certainly aware that there was not a proper and sufficient accommodation for the clergyman of this parish, and his wish was that that want should be supplied. I have just been over the house, and am satisfied; for, as a monument, a more appropriate one could not have been erected and, as a dwelling, a more convenient and commodious one could not have been conceived, and great credit is due to the architect who so admirably designed it. I will say no more at present than to thank Mr Mortlock for his exertions in this act, and, as he said he was anxious in this matter to follow my father in his liberality, I think I may say he has succeeded doing so." The noble Duke then turned to the Rev J Steavenson, the Incumbent of All Saints parish, and on presenting the key, with possession of the Rutland Memorial House, to him and the succeeding clergy of the parish for ever, said. "I beg to present you with this key and residence and sincerely hope that you will live many years therein, with health to enjoy it." Mr Steavenson, in a brief and suitable speech, thanked his Grace and the subscribers, and the company separated. His Grace left for London by the four o'clock train.

This new parsonage described above stood on the site of the new police station in Vicarage Road next to All Saints School.

25th June 1859

The Measles – This disease is now prevalent among children in this neighbourhood, to several of whom it has proved fatal. Parents ought to be careful in every case, and see that the child affected, or about to be affected has proper medicine and is kept comfortably warm.

2nd July 1859

Scarcity of Water – Great inconvenience has been experienced by the tradesman and the public in consequence of the clouds of dust so frequently driven about in this town and the streets were never known to be in so bad a condition for want of being watered. Complaints have been made but the authorities are unable to remove the dust nuisance for fear of exhausting the already limited supply of water. The street watering has been discontinued since the spring meetings.

23rd July 1859

Crinoline Accident – On Tuesday week, a young woman, named Baldwin, was passing rather quickly over the pavement in the front street, when she caught her foot in one of her hoops, and was thrown down with considerable violence upon her face, which was very seriously cut and disfigured.

The full skirt of the crinoline was introduced into fashion from Paris in 1854 fitted over a frame, firstly made of stiff horse hair, then steel hoops to keep the shape. When the fashion for the crinoline passed, the machines used to braid the hoops became redundant. At the same time the electrical industry was looking for ways of insulating single wires, so that they could be bound into multi-conductor cables, in great demand by the telegraph and telephone companies. The Manchester based firm of Glover & Co Ltd were quick to see the chance for the re-use of the old machines and with modification successfully bound braiding on to electrical conductors.

23rd July 1859

Robbery – One evening last week a quantity of wearing apparel was stolen from the Woolpack Inn, in this town, the possession of which were traced to a loose character named Nathan Fitch, of Cheveley, a pensioner of the Royal Marines. He was apprehended on Friday, and conveyed to the Police station at Mildenhall.

6th August 1859

Fatal Accident – On Wednesday evening last as a lad about ten years of age, son of William Wright, postman between Newmarket and Wickhambrook, was swinging with some other lads upon the premises of Mr Samuel Rogers, he was by some means wounded in the neck, and back of the head, by the tines of a stable fork, which penetrated the spine of the neck. He was conveyed home immediately and notwithstanding the unremitting attention of Mr Faircloth and other medical assistance he died about an hour after the accident. There are various reports as to the manner in which the accident was occasioned, many believing that the boys were playfully trying to catch his neck between the tines as he was swinging, but of course all the facts will come out at the inquest which was fixed for Friday.

20th August 1859

Scarcity of Water – The supply of water in this neighbourhood is becoming more and more exhausted, and many with difficulty obtain sufficient for their cattle and domestic purposes. Many of the deep wells have been dry during the summer, while the shallow ones here had plenty of water, but these are now beginning to fail, and many of the good ponds are again empty. Several wells have been bored and deepened, but the water arising therefrom is also exhausted.

27th August 1859

Newmarket – *Apprehension of a Forger of Base Money* – As a young policeman, son of Mr R Petchy, gamekeeper, in this neighbourhood, belonging to the St Ives Force, was walking through the High Street, in this town, on Tuesday last, in plain cloths, being on a visit to his friends, he unhesitatingly pounced upon a vendor of earthenware, and conveyed him to the police station, on suspicion of being the person described in the *Police Gazette*, who had been committed on a charge of passing bad money in various parts of Derbyshire. The facts of the case are that in the spring of last year, an itinerant vendor of cheap mirrors, named Thomas Kerry, was detected in passing bad money, and on being searched several counterfeit florins were found upon him, and he was accordingly committed for trail; at the Quarter Sessions at Derby, but ultimately allowed bail. At the time appointed his father and uncle, who were his sureties, appeared in Court, but the prisoner himself was *non est*, and consequently their recognisances were estreated. Some time afterwards he visited St Ives in a different line of business, when fancying the police were about apprehending him he disappeared, and nothing more was seen or heard of him till Tuesday last, when Petchy, remembering the description of the man, took him at all hazards, and singularly enough he was the very man for whom the police had so long been on the alert. The superintendent of the Derby Police Force was appraised of his apprehension, and on Friday last two officers arrived and conveyed him to that town. Much praise is due to Petchy for the display in this case.

3rd September 1859

Accident on the Railway – On Tuesday last, a serious accident to a stoker upon the goods train, named James Murphy, by which he very narrowly escaped with his life. It appears that the mid-day goods train had just emerged from the tunnel near the Newmarket station, when Murphy proceeded to oil the works of the engine while in motion, and on leaving the tender for that purpose, he by some means, lost his hold of the railing, and was precipitated with considerable violence, his body coming in severe contact with the ground, and his head striking, it is supposed, the brickwork; but, fortunately, he was thrown in a direction from the railway, otherwise he would have been crushed to atoms by the train. When picked up he was unconscious, and blood was flowing copiously from his head, and for nearly twenty minutes it could not be clearly decided whether he was alive or dead. A surgeon was soon in attendance, and rendered him all the assistance necessary, and during the day was removed to Cambridge.

10th September 1859

School Treat – On Thursday last, the children of the schools of St Mary's and All Saints parishes, in this town, enjoyed their annual fete in the park grounds of W P Isaacson, Esq., when, through the kindness of the managers, the Union school children were invited to participate in the fun and good things prepared, and upwards of 300 were bountifully regaled with plumcake, bread and butter, and tea. This treat is got up by voluntary subscription, and admirably managed by the Revs. J Isaacson and Steavenson, who, with Mrs Isaacson, Mrs Steavenson, and other ladies of the town, were anxious to promote the comfort of the juvenile company. As the funds would not permit of the usual engagement of a band, this portion of the treat was dispensed with, but fortunately an itinerant company of musicians came into the town, and were kindly engaged by W P Isaacson, Esq., and greatly augmented the pleasures of the scene. After tea, the usual presents for general good conduct were distributed with appropriate remarks. The children then indulged in various rustic sports till the shades of evening had set in.

The Marquis of Exeter's covered ride, 1840

10th September 1859

The Turf ~ Newmarket is about to lose one of its oldest patrons. Lord Exeter, who has now for some time removed his horses from the town, has given instructions for the sale of his house, known as Foley House, and his paddock, cottages, and training stables.
The eccentric Lord Exeter lived at Foley House, where he built the first covered ride for exercising horses in the 1840s. He had the habit of ignoring others out of doors walking from one end of the High Street to the other without acknowledging any who saluted him. On relinquishing racing he sold his property to Mr Simpson, the banker at Diss. Silzer

Garden Robberies ~ For some time past, several gardens in the town have been visited by nocturnal marauders, who have either wilfully damaged the flowers, etc., or carried off portions of fruit, and on Friday, the 2nd inst., about four o'clock, Inspector Steggles, of the Suffolk force, detected a man named William Laite, formerly a blacksmith, in the act of stealing potatoes from a garden of the Rev. Jas. Isaacson, Rector of St Mary's parish. He was taken before S G Benyon, Esq., and committed for three months.

1st October 1859

Scarcity of Water – The scarcity of water in many parts of this neighbourhood is becoming more and more serious. The poor may be seen hunting out bye places and ponds, at a considerable distance, for water, which, when obtained, even in small quantities, is not fit for cattle, much less for domestic purposes. Where there is a supply in villages, it is eked out with studied economy. Nine out of ten wells and ponds are dry, the owners of wells are repeatedly deepening them, at considerable expense, for a new supply, which continues, in many instances, but for a short time.

15th October 1859

A somewhat impudent but mysterious robbery was effected here on Tuesday morning, at the Rutland Arms. It appears that during the week, Mr Huffan, agent to Baron Rothschild, stopped as usual, when he comes to the races, at this hotel. About six o'clock, on Tuesday morning, he awoke, got out of bed, but on consulting his repeater, found he was an hour before his usual time of rising, and resolved to return to his bed, but before doing so, unlocked the bedroom door; at this time his pocket book containing about £60 in notes and gold, and some valuable memorandas was lying on the dressing table. After about an hour's sleep he awoke again, and on preparing to dress found the pocket-book and its contents had vanished, the thief having entered the room and abstracted it therefrom, doubtless, a very short time before he got out of bed, as the bedroom door was left ajar. It can hardly be questioned that the offence was committed by some one connected with the establishment, but at this busy time so many strange servants are employed, that it would be difficult to determine who is the thief. The police are making an investigation which is not unlikely to result in the arrest of the guilty person.

The Baron Meyer de Rothschild came to Newmarket in 1857, he bought the remains of the royal palace, Palace House Mansion, from the Golding family in 1867. Today it houses the Tourist Information Office. He died in 1874 at the age of 55. His daughter married Lord Rosebery who became prime minister. He lived at Primrose House in the High Street.

The Theatre – The Theatre is now open here with a select number of *artistes* connected with the Drury Lane Company, under the management of Mr Templeton; that fine old comedian, Mr Tilbury, a popular favourite in Cambridge, and indeed everywhere he appears, being stage manager and one of the corps. We are glad to find that the season has been so successful, that the company will be induced to come again. The performances have been patronised by Sir R Peel, Sir G Armitage, Sir W Booth, Lord Canterbury, and many noblemen and gentlemen of distinction.

31st December 1859

A Singing Mouse – A little mouse has been caught in the shop of Mrs Rogers, chemist, which sings in very musical notes, resembling the canary, and sometimes the linnet. Mr Bell, the manager of the business, had frequently heard the little creature singing under the floor of his office, and one morning last week it sat in the corner of the room and whistled several pleasing imitations of the feathered tribe, and allowed itself to be taken without resistance. The little fellow was put into a snug cage, and placed in the public shop; but on Monday last he died.

Arthur Rogers, chemist and druggist, and agent to Phoenix Fire Insurance Company. High Street. PO Directory 1864

1860

7th January 1860

Accident – One night last week, as Mr Chas Clarke, the master of the Union, was passing from one portion of the house to the other, his candle went out, and on mistaking one door for that of another and fancying he was entering a room he unfortunately fell down a flight of stairs, and received considerable injury to his head and arm. He is now recovering.

District Volunteer Mounted Rifle Corps – In pursuance of the resolution passed at a public meeting at Cambridge on the 24th ult., the local committee of the Newmarket district held a conference at the Subscription Room, Newmarket on the 3rd inst. Isaac Herbert Wilkinson, Esq. of Hare Park, in the chair, when the Chairman having fully explained the purpose of the meeting, subscription lists were opened for the effective and honorary members and for general donations. The best feeling prevailed at the conference, and it seemed to be the unanimous opinion that a fully and efficient corps would be raised for the district.

Due to a perceived threat from Napoleon III of France, May 1859 saw the formation of volunteer corps of riflemen, under the auspices of the government. By the end of the year many thousands were enrolled in all parts of the country. On 7th March 1860, 2,500 volunteer officers were presented to the Queen, after which they dined together, the Duke of Cambridge occupying the chair.

14th January 1860

Town Rifle Corps – There is a probability of an Infantry Rifle Corps being established amongst the tradesmen and others who could not make it convenient to join the mounted corps.

Unemployed Labourers – we are sorry to report that in several of our villages, members of the labouring families have [for some weeks past] been in a most deplorable condition, in consequence of not being able to obtain employment. In one extensive village we were informed that between twenty and thirty men and boys were out of employment at one time, in another from ten to fifteen, and so in proportion to the extent of the parish; and rather than be in the Union, of which so many have a dread, they would contrive to struggle on, from day to day, with one or two stinted meals of potatoes or turnips, and in some instances a piece of bread once a day, obtained on credit till they may be employed, when, of course, they will have to eke out their day wages for the purpose of making up the instalments of their debts. It is evident that farming labour is very dull at this season, but would it not be to the advantage of a parish, where there is a surplus of working hands, to make stone and gravel pits, in which those men might be employed, rather than buy road materials from pits in a neighbouring parish?

A Boy Sentenced to twenty-one Days' Imprisonment for Throwing a Snowball – At the Petty Sessions on Tuesday last, a boy named Tweed, of Cheveley, was charged with having thrown a snowball, and struck a young woman names Elizabeth Bailey, upon the face. At the time the offence was committed the lad's father gave complainant's father permission to flog him, but the mother objected to the punishment, and hinted that she should proceed against Bailey if he flogged her boy; consequently the case was decided by the Magistrates, who fined the lad 2s.6d, with 16s costs, or 21 days' imprisonment. He was locked up till night, when to save him from the disgrace of a prison a tradesman of the village paid the money, which the parents agreed to re-pay by instalments. We understand that the money has been made up by subscriptions.

21st January 1860

Rifle Corps – We last week reported that there was a probability of an Infantry Rifle Corps being established independently of the mounted corps which many tradesmen and small occupiers of land could not join, and before the paper was published it was found that the advocates of such a corps had actually started in the right way to ensure success. A notice was issued, and a document explaining the object was drawn out and placed upon a table in the Corn Exchange on Tuesday last, for the signatures of those who might be disposed to join the infantry, as well as lists of the names of the Committee and members of the mounted corps. A few names were put down for the infantry, and we have no doubt that a large number will soon join were the rules and regulations fully explained to the public, but from the many enquiries made by those looking over the lists it was palpable that the fact of having to purchase uniforms and accoutrements, and the want of a Committee of gentlemen, like those who have interested themselves in the mounted corps, caused considerable hesitation in the minds of those who would enrol themselves. We have since heard that the formation of those corps is likely to be taken in hand by some of the leading gentlemen in the county.

Amateur Theatricals – During the winter months some young gentlemen of this own formed themselves into a class of theatrical performers, and by study and perseverance soon attained to a sufficient proficiency to perform before an audience of their friends and neighbours. Last week they gave three entertainments, *Robert Macaire* and *The Eaton Boy*, in which Messrs F Hammond, J F Arnall, and Wm. Norville took the principal parts, and gave unlimited satisfaction to a large company.

18th February 1860

A Pauper's Funeral – On Thursday last, the body of a poor man was being conveyed from Newmarket Union for interment at Gazeley, when, on ascending Moulton Hill, the door of the hearse became unfastened, the coffin slid out upon the ground, and the driver, all unconscious, would have proceeded on his way without the corpse, had not some labourers, who happened to witness the occurrence, called to him and assisted to replace the coffin within the hearse.

3rd March 1860

The Cemetery – The Cemetery chapels have been duly licensed and registered for the performance of the burial service, which was accordingly read therein for the first time last week.

Public Hall – This Hall has been engaged by the Rev J Smith, jun., of Newmarket, for the four Sundays in March, for special religious services for the million, for which it has been duly registered. Both Churchmen and Dissenters are invited by public placards to exert themselves in the promotion of this cause.
In a further report of 31st March 1860 Rev Jas. Smith, Jun., was described as 'resident Baptist Minister'.

The Hurricane – On Tuesday last, the wind rose to a perfect hurricane, and made considerable havoc among trees in many of the plantations in this neighbourhood, and completely uncovered every stack exposed to its fury, and caused much damage to houses and other buildings. Several large and ancient trees were blown down, and in two plantations adjoining the Park at Cheveley, between 400 and 500 trees were either broken off or torn up by the roots, and from what we have heard, equal ravages have been experienced in other plantations. Houses have been partially unroofed, and chimney pots were blown down in various places. A large chimney fell with tremendous force upon the Wellington Inn, Newmarket, and forced itself through the roof into the rooms below; but fortunately, no one was in the rooms at the time. Several stacks have been completely overturned, and straw and corn were seen rolling across the country in fantastic wreaths, until stopped by some hedge where it might be seen in the same manner as drifted snow. On the following day, farmers were busily employed in restacking, raking up the scattered corn or straw, and fresh thatching. It was with considerable difficulty that many reached the market on Tuesday, and one gentleman informed us that his horse was repeatedly brought to a standstill, and at time it appeared as if the animal was really lifted off its legs by the violence of the wind, which is described as the strongest remembered for many years.

10ᵗʰ March 1860

Sporting Telegraph – Until last Spring meeting a very annoying and dangerous system of transmitting the results of each race from the course to the Railway Telegraph and other necessary offices in the town, by desperate riding upon horseback through the principal street was practised, and afterwards discontinued for the safer and quicker mode of transmission by the corresponding numbers of the winning horses upon the racing lists held up by a party stationed upon the course and received by others at the entrance to the town, who in like manner displayed them to the person stationed with a telescope at the Telegraph-office. This system has worked very well in clear weather, but has proved to be fallacious in dull and misty weather, when the numbers cannot be distinctly seen. To obviate this difficulty and inconvenience, a subterranean telegraph from the course, where an office would be erected, to the Electric Telegraph-office in the town is in contemplation. We understand that arrangements are being made to carry out the scheme immediately, and that the company are only awaiting the permission of the Duke of Rutland for laying down the wires.
The results of the races had to be transmitted from the course to the town by express riders, the service being run by a man named Wright. The only electric telegraph was at the railway station, and the names of the first three horses were brought in by mounted messenger. It was a case of, "Out of the way! The express is coming." That service, however, came to be beaten by that of another firm, who had men stationed on

Cambridge Hill with a telescope, and big placards on which the names of the winners were written in characters big enough to be caught by another telescope on Queensbury paddock wall, where a cob would be in readiness to dash off to the telegraph office at the old station. (Memories of Robert Edward Rodrigo, 1842-1924)

17ᵗʰ March 1860

Public Hall – Religious Services – The Rev Jas. Smith, of Newmarket, gave his first course of a series of religious services and lectures in this hall on Sunday, the 4ᵗʰ inst. The company was very large and strictest order was observed. This being a novel move in this town, scores, in addition to those of Mr Smith's denomination, were present, and the service was conducted in a plain and unassuming manner. Mr Smith gave his second service on Sunday last, when a very numerous congregation assembled. We have been informed that the opening of the Hall for the purpose of religious services has been the means of keeping many from their usual rendezvous, the public tap-rooms; and that on the two evenings in question, instead of going to the public-house, several were observed to be wending their way to the hall and, after the service, to return quietly to their homes. The services will be continued during Lent.

Accident – As Mr Thomas Morley and Mr Bain were returning from Newmarket to Soham on Tuesday night, and when opposite to Phantom Cottage (the night being very dark), the wheel of their gig came in contact with that of Mr William Collett's of Quy. The former were not unseated, but Mr Collett and his sister were precipitated to the ground; both shafts of Mr Collett's gig were broken, and the horse ran off to Newmarket. We are glad to learn that neither Mr or Miss Collett sustained any serious injury.

24ᵗʰ March 1860

The Sporting Telegraph – We understand the Electric and International Telegraph Company have obtained the Duke of Rutland's permission to lay down the telegraph wires under the heath, and that the telegraph will be in readiness for the transmission of messages on the first day of the ensuing meetings.

31 March 1860

The Rifle Corps – From what we have heard, these corps, the mounted and foot, which at first promised so well, have not increased for several weeks; in fact, we are told that mot a single man has been enrolled in the foot, and not more than one (if any) in the mounted corps, since the meeting on the 9th January. The gentlemen of the mounted corps will shortly receive their uniform, which will be a light mixed grey, similar to the Cambridge University corps, and arrangements are being made for the commencement of drill as soon as circumstances will permit. We understand that practice will be conducted on foot, under a sergeant-major of a cavalry regiment, but the ground has not yet been selected. The race-course has been recommended as the most convenient, but the permission of the Jockey Club must first be obtained. A safer and more secluded practice-ground in the 'Devils Ditch' west of the course, has been suggested, where a natural butt is formed at the gap, with a range of upwards of a quarter of a mile, with several feet of embankment on both sides.

7th April 1860

Rifle Corps – The Newmarket Rifle Corps assembled in the Park Grounds on Tuesday last and went through the drill in good order under Sergeant Hazelwood of the Grenadier Guards, of Cambridge. Every member spoke in high terms of the manner in which the Sergeant performed his duty.

The New Telegraph – The sporting telegraph from the course to the town is now about being complete, the office being at the stand, and will be working for the transmission of racing messages at the opening of the Spring Meeting on Monday next.

14th April 1860

Daring Robbery – On Monday last a rather impudent robbery was committed in the Palace, occupied by Mr Godding, a training-groom of this town, in the following manner – During the afternoon, as the servant was proceeding upstairs, she met two respectably dressed women, named Boyce and Bacon, both of this town, coming from one of the bedrooms, but not knowing them, and thinking they were her mistress's friends, accordingly made room for them to pass. At this moment, Mr Godding's mother came to the stairs also, and politely made way for the intruders, whom she, on the other hand, took to be friends of the servant. As soon as these bold women had

left the house, Mrs Godding very naturally asked who the girl's friends were, and was answered that she, the girl, thought they were her mistress's friends. The girl at once appraised her mistress of what had taken place, and on going up-stairs, Mrs Godding and her mother-in-law found the rooms in a state of confusion and on searching, discovered that several articles had been stolen. The women were sent for and asked what they were after in the house? When they replied that they merely went in to look at some furniture (which curiously enough had been sold off a week or two previously) and offered to be searched. Of course they had disposed of the stolen property before they were brought back, therefore nothing was found upon them, with the exception of one of Mrs Godding's pocket handkerchiefs, secreted in one of their muffs, which they had forgotten to leave with the other property. They are remanded until Tuesday next.
1861 Census, Palace, James Godding, 40, training groom; his wife Jessie, 24; daughter Elizabeth, 4; son George, 3, and an unnamed son, 13 days. The female servants were Ann Price, 40, cook; Rosa Bailey, 17, housemaid; and Mary Meacham, 48, nurse.

21st April 1860

Accident – A little boy of the name Count, of this town, was run over by a cart in the front street on Tuesday afternoon and had his leg broken.
1861 Census, Joseph Count, 17, and Frank Count, 10, stable boys to Mr Arnull, Bury Road. William Count, 15, stable boy to Mr Stebbings, Station Road.

5th May 1860

The Foot Rifle Corps – This corps only existed to flicker inertly for a short time, and then die a natural death. Two or three names were added to the list when the movement was first suggested, but afterwards no addition could be made, and every one appeared indifferent in the matter when the corps was disbanded.

12th May 1860

St Mary's Church – It appears that there are faculty pews in the church which have been recognised for many years as entirely distinct from the free sittings, and that when the restoration of the church was contemplated, the owners of those pews gave the Rector and Churchwardens full liberty to alter them according to the proposed arrangements. In making the alterations, the pew attached to Rockingham House was converted into free sittings, and some ladies having purchased that house in expectation of having the pew, great dissatisfaction of expressed at its removal; but whether the complaint is well founded must of course depend upon whether the faculty was a good one, and if so, whether the late possessor of the house actually relinquished it. If he did so, and did not make known the fact to the purchasers of the house, the complaint lies not against the church officers, but against the vendor.

28th July 1860

Human Bones Discovered – Last week as some men were emptying one of the main receptacles of the refuse of the town, a human skull and some bones were found deeply embedded in the soil, which, to all appearance, had not been removed for some years. This, of course, brought to mind the sudden disappearance from the town of a young woman named Wright, who has never been heard of since, and was thought to be murdered, and an inquest was spoken of, but the examination of the bones by Dr Mead rendered further inquiry unnecessary. He pointed out and explained that the skull-bone was that of a male about 30 years of age, and had, in his opinion from its decayed appearance, been in the soil upwards of fifty years. The other bones were those of some animal, the name of which he did not at the time remember, but similar ones might be found in public museums. It certainly appears strange that the skull-bone of a human being should be found deposited in the soil of the town with the bones of a strange animal, and by what means they reached the spot in which they were found remains a mystery.
George Borwick Mead, surgeon, High Street. PO Directory, 1864. The 1867 Newmarket Directory implies Dr Mead lived next door to the Crown Inn.

11th August 1860

Accident – On Saturday last a little boy, son of Mr Bartholomew, of the Crown, was accidentally knocked down by a butcher's cart, which passed over his neck and severely injured him. It was at first thought it would prove fatal, but we are glad to say that he is now recovering.

A Man Substituted for a Horse – Last week, a novel scene of a man yoked to a large four-wheeled chaise, which he was drawing through the town, rather surprised those who witnessed it. He was stripped with the exception of his trousers and shirt, and bareheaded, and appeared much distressed, with the perspiration running down his face upon the ground, and on stopping to enquire the road to Wickhambrook, he said he had already drawn the carriage from Cambridge that morning, and then had about ten miles further to go. He had nothing over his shoulders to assist him in drawing, but pulled the whole weight by his hands. It appears he is in the habit of drawing gigs and carriages from a manufacture, to various parts of the County.

25th August 1860

School Treat – On Thursday last, the children of the schools of the two parishes had their annual fête in Queensbury paddocks, tea, plum cake, etc. being provided. The treat is under the management of the ladies of the town. After tea, the usual field games were started, but unfortunately a sharp shower put a stop to them for a time.

1st September 1860

Elnathan Flatman, better known as 'Nat', the celebrated jockey, dies at Newmarket on the 20th inst, at the age of 50. He was born at Helton in Suffolk, and at the age of 14 went to Newmarket, where he gradually rose from the lowest position in the line of business he had adopted. His death was the termination of suffering caused by an accident which occurred nearly four years ago. At Newmarket First October Meeting last year, while unsaddling Golden Pippin, he accidentally drew the surcingle over the mare's tail, whereupon she jumped forward, kicking him severely on the left rib and abdomen, fracturing one rib and causing severe internal injuries. The broken rib, it was found, had penetrated the lung. The mortal remains of Mr Flatman were interred on Monday last in the churchyard of All Saints, a licence for the purpose having been obtained, and the great respect in which he was held was fully evidenced by the large attendance of the most respectable inhabitants, trainers, etc. On the occasion Mr C F Frye presided at the organ and the Dead March from *Saul* formed part of the funeral service.
1861 Census. Susan Flatman, widow, 48; daughters Ellen 21, Nancy 15, Phillis 13; and sons Nathaniel 19 and John 17, living in Station Road.

The Rifle Corps – We understand that the mounted corps, which has made considerable and satisfactory progress in drill and horse exercise, have withdrawn from further practice till after harvest, when it is expected their numbers will be augmented, and rifle practice be commenced. The infantry corps is going on favourably, and will shortly be brought out of their initiatory lessons in drill. The original proposition that the infantry should be called the Suffolk Corps has been overruled, but it must be understood that volunteers will be admitted from both Cambridgeshire and Suffolk. Young men in the town and neighbourhood are very anxious to join, and doubtless as soon as the regulations are made public the numbers will rapidly increase.

22nd September 1860

Removal of the Post Office – This office for the last few years has not been located quite so centrally as could have been wished for, but it has this week been removed to a much more convenient and central part of the town, immediately opposite Mr Simpson's, printer and bookseller, in the High Street, to the premises where it was situated many years past.

The Post Office was next to the Star Inn [see August 1856]. Mr Simpson's shop was between Wellington Street and the Greyhound Inn, later the Carlton.

29th September 1860

The Small Pox – For some time reports have been freely circulating in the neighbourhood that the small-pox was raging through the town, and that some very bad cases existed, till persons from the surrounding villages began to be afraid to venture there upon their ordinary business. These reports, we are happy to inform the public, proved, by an official enquiry by the Board of Health, to be considerably exaggerated, though there certainly were two or three cases of a mild description in the back part of the town, which through caution and proper treatment were prevented from spreading. The inhabitants are indebted to the surgeons of the town for the tact they displayed in checking the disease, for wherever symptoms were suspected or appeared the patient was most judiciously kept in quarantine till all danger had disappeared. We are directed to say that all who have been affected are rapidly approaching convalescence, and that no danger is now to be apprehended.

6th October 1860

The Potato Disease – The potato disease is getting worse and worse in this neighbourhood, for not only are the undug potatoes very bad, but those which have been selected as good have, in many instances after having been laid up for a week or two, gradually turned black and rotten. Many of the poor have not got a sufficient quantity off their allotments of a quarter of an acre of ground, to supply them with the seed for the next planting season. The crop which was formerly so great an advantage to a poor family, must now be dispensed with, for where good ones are to be found the prices asked are really enormous, ranging from 10s. to £1.4s. per sack. Some have been sold here at 10s. a bushel, and of not an extraordinary quality.

31st October 1860

Accident – As Mr Baxter, hay and straw dealer, of Newmarket was driving upon the Bury road, on Friday, the 5th inst., his horse took fright and started off suddenly, turning the vehicle over upon a stone heap, and seriously cutting him about the head, and otherwise injuring him in the body.

1861 Census. John Baxter, 45, hay merchant; wife, Mary Ann, 33; and son, William 8. Living at Turf Terrace.

29th December 1860

Annual Christmas Presents – On Friday week, According to ancient custom, a considerable quantity of meat, bread, and money, was given out at the National School to all the poor families of the town. The Rev J Steavenson of All Saints parish gave a liberal gift of coals to all the widows, widowers, and necessitous persons in this part of town. B Colman, Esq., merchant, gave joints of meat to his workmen and servants; and other gentlemen and tradesmen of the town have likewise contributed to the domestic comforts of their dependents and poorer neighbours.

Barnard Colman, merchant, High Street. PO Directory 1964. 1861 Census. Barnard Colman, 43, malster corn and seed merchant, residing at Shag Bag. [Shag Bag, now Sackville Street, got its name from the bag used to carry fighting cocks]. The Newmarket Directory 1867. Colman, corn merchant, in Station Road, near the railway station.

Bibliography

Newmarket, its Sport and Personalities. Frank Siltzer 1923

The Victorian Countryside, Vols. 1 & 2. G. E. Mingay 1981

The Changing face of Newmarket, 1600-1760. Peter May 1984

A Look at Five Newmarket Buildings. Joan Shaw 2002

The History of Newmarket and its Surrounding Areas Vol. 1 & 2. Sandra Easom 2000

Victoria County History of Cambridgeshire. Vol. 10

Newmarket: a photographic history. Joan Shaw 2001

Collins Dictionary of British History. 1997

A History of Newmarket General Hospital. Dick Heasman 1996

The Life and Times of the Great Eastern Railway. Harry Parr and Adrian Grey 1991

The Mildenhall Branch. Peter Paye 1988

Red Coat. Richard Holmes 2002.

Victorian Cambridge, Josiah Chater's Diaries. Enid Porter 1975

A Postal History of Cambridge. Muggleton 1970.

East Anglia Postal History Bulletins.

The Newmarket, Bury, Thetford & Cromer Road. Charles Harper 1904

John Gully and his times. Bernard Darwin 1935

Soho Past. Richard Tames 1994

Labouring Life in the Victorian Countryside. Pamela Horn 1976

A Tradition Unshared: a History of Cambridge Town Cricket 1700-1890. Willie Sugg 2002

Dictionary of Architects of Suffolk Buildings, 1800-1914. Brown Haward Kindred 1991

Memories of Robert Edward Rodrigo, 1842-1924. Papers in Newmarket Local History Society Archive

Josselyn, J 40
Jullien's Band 45
Keane, Lord 44
Kendall, Mr 13
Kennet 55,60
Kent, John 43
Kentford 60
Kerry, Thomas 79
Key, Colonel 72
King, Edward 49
Kings, Mr 44
Kingston House 16-20,50
Kingston Passage 50
Kingston Square 45
Kirtlinge Tower 39
Kitchener, Mr 58
Kitchner, Mr 41
Knipe, Revd. 76
Laite, William 80
Lamb inn 57
Landwade 10
Last, Miss 14
Le Pla, William 59,64
Leach, Richard 29
Lee, Mr 38
Leigh, Colonel 11
Linwood, John 53
Literary Institution 44,48,66,73
Long, H A 74
Loose, Mr 61
Lovick, John 56
Mail coaches 1,14,17,20
Mainprice, John 56
Manners, George 24,28,44,66
Manning, James 45
Marham, Mr 44
Market Lane 57
Market Place 18,22,28,33,56
Market Street 54
Marquis of Granby inn 56
Marrow, Josiah 40
Marshal, Robert 69
Marshall, Ben 4
Marshall, Josiah 5
Marshall, Lambert 4
Marson, Charles 27
Marson, Julia 27
Marson, Superintendent 51
Martin, John 56
Mason, John 51
Matthews, Tom 71
Mead, George B 76
Mellish, Colonel 9
Mendham, John 5
Mendoza, Daniel 8
Militia 46,54,59
Mill Hill 5,12,18-20,24,26,35,51,57,62,68
Mills, Mr 38
Mirtlock, Edmund 25
Mole, 'Pet' 31

Moody, Mr 26,42
Moody, Thomas 14
Moody, Tyrell 66,69
Moore, F R 17
Mortlock, E 77
Mosgrove, Mr 22
Mould, James 62
Moulton 4,18-9,26,30,38,46, 50,60,77
Mount Pleasant 11
Munnings, P 75
Murphy, James 79
Nash, John 11
National Schoolroom 74
Naylor, Mr 31
Neale, Mr 60
Nelson, Robert 20
New Town 43,71
Newman, Chappel B 40
Newman, Mr 75
Newmarket Union *see* Workhouse
Newton, Thomas 44
Nickoldson, 'Butcher' 31
Norton, Taylor & Kendall 13
Nunn, Mr 15
Nunnery 10
Odd Fellows 44,65
Old Palace *see* Royal Palace
Orme, Puglist 41
Osbaldeston, George 14
Pack, James R 19
Page, Frederick 18,23,38,58,76
Palace House Mansion 11,81
Palmer, John 57
Palmer, William 62
Panton House 9,54,72
Panton, Thomas 9,40
Paradise Row 19
Paris, Eliza 75
Parker, Mr 51,65
Parkinson, Robert 56
Parrot, James 55
Pars, Albertus 12
Partridge, G A 54,62
Parvis, Arthur 75
Pask, Thomas 58
Pavis, Charles 63
Pearson, Samuel 56
Peck, G F 34
Peck, J M 38,58,62,67
Peck, Thomas 37
Peel, Robert 75,81
Pellew, E 74
Pemberton & Fiske 10
Pennington, Mr 62
Petchy, R 79
Petingall, 'Pet' 39
Phillips, Charles 19,22,24,27, 29,37-8,58,64
Phillips, Mr 44
Pierce, William 9
Pigot, R 44